P9-CEI-282

EARN THE
RIGHT TO WIN

EARN THE RIGHT TO WIN

HOW SUCCESS IN ANY FIELD STARTS
WITH SUPERIOR PREPARATION

TOM COUGHLIN

with David Fisher

PORTFOLIO/PENGUIN

PORTFOLIO/PENGUIN
Published by the Penguin Group
Penguin Group (USA) Inc., 375 Hudson Street,
New York, New York 10014, USA

USA | Canada | UK | Ireland | Australia New Zealand | India | South Africa | China

Penguin Books Ltd, Registered Offices: 80 Strand, London WC2R 0RL, England
For more information about the Penguin Group, visit penguin.com

ISBN: 978-159-184612-3

Printed in the United States of America
10 9 8 7 6 5 4 3 2 1

Book design by Alissa Amell

ALWAYS LEARNING   PEARSON

This book is dedicated to my wife, Judy; our children, Keli, Tim, Brian, and Kate; and their spouses, Chris, Andrea, Susie, and Chris. My children have always been my greatest supporters. They have been there in good times and through the bad times. Now, as their children, our eleven beautiful grandchildren, are introduced to the New York Giants and professional football, we find great joy in sharing many wonderful adventures with them. Professionally, there is nothing that compares with raising the Lombardi Trophy. Personally, one of my great thrills has been to share the raising of the Lombardi with Judy and our children and grandchildren.

CONTENTS

A Winning Relationship

I had been playing for the New York Giants for more than a decade when Tom Coughlin was named head coach in 2004. Tom has since been recognized as one of the greatest coaches in NFL history, but at the beginning, our relationship was tough: I hated him. Hate is a strong word, but that's the way I felt. He was hard on everybody; he seemed to be overly concerned about petty things that made no difference, like being five minutes early to every meeting, wearing the same color practice jerseys, having your helmet strap buttoned up even when we weren't in practice. The players didn't think that he was treating us as professionals. He also wasn't open to any discussion about his tactics. His attitude was, This is what it is and this is what it's going to be. Period. After my first season playing for him I didn't know if I wanted to come back.

While I was making my decision, I happened to hear a Coldplay song, "Clocks." There is a line in that song that caused me to pause: "Am I part of the cure, or am I part of the disease?" I thought about that, and I had to wonder, Was I doing what I could to improve the situation or was I making it worse? I could either continue rebelling and fighting against him, or I could decide that those things were insignificant and just do my job to the best of my ability and see what happened.

I started to look at Tom Coughlin differently. What are his objectives? I wondered. What are his goals? Is he just trying to make us miserable with all these rules? Clearly his objective was to win. I thought about that and realized, Okay, we have that in common. What else do we have in common? It turned out that there were a lot of things: We both liked to do things the right way, we both were hard workers, we both enjoyed being leaders, and we both loved what we were fortunate enough to be doing.

When I began adding it all up, I realized, You know what? Maybe I haven't been seeing this guy the right way. Maybe there's more to this guy than I originally believed.

At that same time Tom's wife, Judy, must have been listening to the same Coldplay song, because apparently she told him that he had to make some changes too. I think that was harder for him than it was for us. But he tried. At first it was strange. He would try to crack jokes and fit in. He stood in front of the team and did jumping jacks. We couldn't figure out what was going on; that definitely wasn't the Tom Coughlin we knew. But eventually we learned that that's exactly who he is.

Probably the biggest change he made was to allow his leaders to be leaders. He formed a leadership council and gave us real decision-making responsibility. When there was a problem, he would tell us, "I need you to handle this." And when we had a suggestion, he listened to us. The more responsibility he gave us, the better the team responded. He didn't demand any less; he demanded the same amount of commitment, focus, the same amount of work, but for the first time there was a feeling that he really cared about us. As a player, when you know that a coach cares about you, you are willing to go above and beyond for him. From a cold and distant figure, he became the man none of us wanted to disappoint.

We learned that there was a purpose behind his system. He didn't enforce the rules because he wanted to catch people and punish them but rather to make sure that everyone was committed to the same purpose. At first we were accountable to the rules, but gradually we became accountable to one another. If my teammate could make the commitment to be at work five minutes early, why couldn't I? Eventually we began to draw pride from getting it done Tom Coughlin's way.

He is not a physically demanding coach. Physically, he was the easiest coach I ever played for. But mentally, I've known few people like him. Once we learned to stop fighting his system, and instead mentally adjusted to it, the little things stopped bothering us. They became habits. What difference did it make if you did it Tom's way rather than the old way? What difference did it make if you got to a meeting five minutes earlier? That allowed us to focus our attention on our opponents. We became a team that knew how to have fun, but also one that understood that when it was time to work, it was definitely time to work. Eventually we developed a unity of purpose, a common commitment to success that took us directly to the Super Bowl.

We never went into a game feeling unprepared. Winning was not all about lifting the most weights or being faster. The way to win was to be mentally prepared to handle the grind, to handle any challenge. Tom Coughlin challenged us from the day he got to New York and prepared us to handle anything that was thrown at us.

He'll never talk about himself this way, which is why I'm writing this. He believes everything that he's done has been accomplished as part of a team. That team mentality is an essential part of the way he coaches. We were all part of something much bigger than any one of us. We were a family. And if anybody in our family needed help, the rest of us were right there to provide it, knowing that people would be there for us. If someone got hurt, someone else would step in, but all of us helped that substitute player until he got comfortable. To me, that's the perfect model for an organization.

Toward the end of my playing career, I would sometimes find myself listening to a younger player complaining about something. "Let me explain something to you," I'd respond.

"You got it easy. We had to break him down. We got the hard Coughlin!" What we learned was that there was a reason for everything he did. That through his experience and the strength of his personality he had created a system that encouraged every player to perform to the best of his ability and to become a winning team. The most difficult thing for us had been to recognize that and then accept it.

And what I eventually discovered was that the lessons I learned from him weren't limited to football, that they were applicable to every aspect of my life. I still draw on them today, and they have made a great difference for me.

I remember being in the locker room after we'd won the Super Bowl, looking around at my teammates and feeling such incredible emotion, knowing what we had been through together. I told them, "I didn't win the Super Bowl. *You* didn't win the Super Bowl. *We* won the Super Bowl. As a *team!*" Tom and I didn't say too much to each other in that locker room; we didn't have to. Both of us knew where we'd started and how far we'd come.

When I look back on our relationship now, I tell people proudly that I love the man. I love him, and if I could, I would play for him any day. And together, we would win.

—*Michael Strahan*

Prepare to Win

*The preparation is where success is truly found. . . . It
was the journey I prized above all else*

—JOHN WOODEN

My father, John Louis Coughlin, was not a man who expressed
his emotions. He was a tough, proud Irishman. We lived in the
small upstate New York town of Waterloo. We always had
enough to eat, the clothes we needed, and a house filled with
love. His values weren't complicated: work hard, give your
best effort, respect other people, and always be honest and fair.
My father was a corporal in the U.S. Army and then worked at
the Seneca Ordnance Depot for the rest of his life. Everything
he did was for his family, and we knew the worst thing we
could possibly do was let him down. During my sophomore
year in high school, I played varsity football. When I came
home one Saturday afternoon after we'd been beaten, he was
waiting at the front door for me. It looked like he'd been standing there for awhile. All he said to me was, "If that's the effort
you're going to give, you probably ought to find something

else to do with your time." That was devastating for me to hear. His message was clear: If you're going to do something, do it to the best of your ability—or don't waste your time. It never happened again.

My mother, Betty Coughlin, was the foundation of our family. She was the most unselfish person I have ever known; everything she did was about helping someone who needed help. I remember having to deliver groceries during a blizzard. I had a job to do, and my parents expected me to do it, storm or no storm. There was too much snow on the ground for me to ride my bike, so my mother drove me house to house in her beat-up car. We couldn't get one of the doors shut , so we tied it closed with a rope. We did what we had to do to get the job done.

Those core values were reinforced every day, grades one through eight, by the Sisters of St. Joseph at St. Mary's parochial school. I served as altar boy from day one; in fact, my family used to call me the master of ceremonies for Mass on Easter and Christmas.

That was my foundation. There was nothing fancy or complicated about it. But everything that I've been fortunate enough to accomplish, in life as well as in football, has been built upon it.

Achieving any goal begins with thorough preparation. That's not a secret: The better you prepare the more likely it is that you'll succeed. My football teams have become known for the emphasis we place on being ready to deal with any situation. We focus on both the big and small details, knowing that it may eventually be the small things that make a big difference. Nothing ever proceeds exactly the way you've anticipated. Success often depends on being prepared for whichever way the ball bounces. We've established a reliable structure that provides the discipline, confidence, and flexibility necessary to deal with challenges without panicking, and to continue to move forward. It's never a question of, Can we do this? but rather, How are we going to do this? Jim Citrin, a top executive recruiter and leadership expert, acknowledged the importance of a reliable structure when he wrote, "To lead people in uncertain times, project a sense of continuity, of having managed through similarly difficult predicaments. Just as panic is contagious, so too is a feeling of calm, which, when it kicks in, can settle the frayed nerves of those around you."

Having a structure to rely on means that when my teams have reached our goal, we can look back at the steps we took along the way to get there. And do it again. There is a great deal of satisfaction in knowing that all the work we've put in, all the late hours, and meetings, and practice, and studying have resulted in success. We didn't get there by luck; we got there by hard work and sacrifice, by following a plan. The phrase we use to describe that feeling is "earning the right to win."

In sports the goal is easy to identify: win. In business or in life the goals may not be so simply defined. But it really doesn't matter, because achieving any goal begins by planning out all of the steps needed to reach it. Chris Pridy, a Giants coaching assistant, and I make schedules, sometimes as far as a year in advance, and the coaches follow them. As one of my assistant coaches pointed out accurately, "In September, I know what time I'm going to be eating lunch the following June." We make lists. We even make lists of the lists that we have to make, so we know how we're going to proceed. We pay close attention to details, often to the details of the details. The whole program focuses on the effective use of time; I have never believed that complaining I don't have enough time is an effective use of my time. The result of this is a reliable, predictable method of getting done everything that needs to be done.

There is a reason for all of this: It works. We know it works, because this is the way my teams have been doing it for more than four decades, and the result has been continuous and substantial success. We've developed organizations from the turf up and coached college and NFL teams to championships doing it exactly this way. It might not be the best method for everyone, but it is the right way for my teams. It is a systematic approach to success based on a great deal of experience. It has certainly evolved as the world has changed, but it has remained consistent with those original values. Even with all the changes we've made, players who were part of the program four decades ago would recognize and feel comfortable in it. If you follow the protocol that we have developed, you will eventually become the best person you are capable of being; you will continue to improve; you'll draw confidence from the system and, as we've seen, that will lead to winning. This method, this system, doesn't just apply to football or competitive sports; it's just as applicable to whatever goals you want to accomplish. Let me warn you, though: You can't cheat, and you can't cut corners, but if you follow this system to the end, you will have earned the right to win. You'll be confident that you have prepared as well as possible to deal with whatever competition or challenge you're facing. You'll know that you're applying the best of your talents and skills to that effort.

Confidence is a self-fulfilling prophecy: The more confidence you have in yourself and your preparation, the better you will perform, and as a result, you'll have even more confidence in the system and your own abilities. And you will continue to succeed.

Earning the right to win is the difference between standing anxiously in front of a door, preparing to go inside for an important meeting, hoping, Oh please don't let me screw this one up, and pushing open that same door and bursting inside, because you know you've done everything possible to prepare for this moment, and, in fact, you're so well prepared, so confident, that you just can't wait to get going.

Earning the right to win means you've dealt with your fear of failure. The fear that you might not succeed—sometimes even before you begin—almost guarantees that you'll fail. Proper preparation will enable you to overcome that fear. The night before a game, even a game as important as the Super Bowl, I sleep well, because I know that my team has prepared both physically and mentally as well as possible. Although I don't always know if we're going to win, I do know that if the team has listened to the messages, themes, and key points that we have emphasized—and responded in practice—we are ready to play well. The knowledge that we have done everything in our power to prepare for that game provides a great deal of confidence. I don't stay awake wondering if there is something else I could have done, or should have done. Preparation creates confidence.

This protocol isn't an especially easy path to follow. At times it requires personal sacrifice. I'm careful never to ask anyone in my organization to do anything that I wouldn't do myself or, most often, haven't already done in the past. Proper preparation requires a lot of hard work over a prolonged period of time. Earning the right to win requires strategic planning, consistency, communication, dedication, and perseverance, but if you make a real commitment to follow through, you won't be surprised when all the effort you put into your objective results in success. Even better is the feeling that comes with it: You'll understand and appreciate the fact that you've earned that success. The changes you've made in how you pursued that objective are part of your life, and they can be applied to almost anything else you want to get done. Simply, if you're the best that you can be, winning will follow.

Success in any endeavor isn't an accident, it's not luck; it's the direct result of hard work. My coaching staff has always emphasized to our players, and admittedly sometimes in loud and harsh language, that if they are not willing to pay the full price to succeed, then they are on the wrong team. Let me take this opportunity to tell you the same thing: If you're not willing to do the work necessary to prepare properly for whatever it is you want to accomplish, please put down this book right now. It isn't for you. You're on the wrong page. Through the seasons of my career I've learned that a team wins playoff football games in January and February because of the things that we did the previous April. Muhammad Ali got it absolutely right when he said, "The fight is won or lost far away from witnesses—behind the lines, in the gym, and out there on the road, long before I dance under those lights."

In 1998, at the beginning of my fourth season as head coach of the Jacksonville Jaguars, we drafted running back Fred Taylor in the first round. Fred eventually had a very successful NFL career, gaining more than eleven thousand

EARN THE RIGHT TO WIN

rushing yards, but there were times in practice during his rookie season that I had to push him harder than he wanted to be pushed. We did have some conflicts. In fact, after I left Jacksonville I read several articles in which he said that he really believed I was trying to kill him during that year.

In the ensuing years Fred and I had spoken a few times. I'd see him on the field when the Giants played his team, and we'd greeted each other politely. But we didn't have a real conversation until after he retired in 2010, when I ran into Fred and his brother at the annual scouting combine in Indianapolis. I was walking through the lobby when I noticed a crowd of people and a little bit of a commotion. As I looked to see what was going on, Fred spotted me. I stopped to say hello, and we started talking. Finally I got around to asking him about that comment. "I didn't understand what you were trying to do then," he said. "I understand it now. I have great respect for you." I explained to him that I had pushed him so hard in order to help him become the best player he was capable of being, to help him develop his natural talents and give him the additional tools he needed to succeed in the NFL. We spoke for a little while longer, and finally he and his brother had to leave for an appointment. I walked with them through the lobby to the elevator. We shook hands and they got into the elevator, but as the doors started closing, Fred said suddenly, "Thank you, I love you." I love you? That was one thing that I wasn't prepared to hear. And just before the

8

doors slammed shut I heard him shout, "And you did try to kill me."

There is a very calculated method to what Fred Taylor once believed was my madness. There is a reason for everything we do. As our players eventually learn, details count. After punter Steve Weatherford had played six NFL seasons with four different teams, we signed him in 2011. I think he was surprised at the level of attention he received from our coaching staff. "Sometimes you don't think a head coach is paying attention to you, because you have such a small portion of the plays in practice," he said. "But Tom Coughlin noticed everything about me when I first got here. . . . One day he told me, 'Yesterday, whenever you hit that one punt out of bounds, you dropped it inside a little bit more, and you were swinging up a little bit more through the ball.' And I was thinking, 'I didn't even think you knew my last name!'

"He stands right by me for every single punt of every single practice, so I know he's there. and even if he wasn't there, I'd still put pressure on myself. But knowing that the head coach is there, you never relax, which is good, because when I get in a game I'm never nervous, I'm never anxious, because I have pressure on me every day at practice. So when I get in a game, and I need to hit an important punt, it's not the first time I've had pressure on myself. It's every day in practice, every punt."

Not every reader of this book is going to bring the same

intense degree of dedication and perseverance to an objective that I do. That's just who I am. I have often described myself as firm, fair, honest, and demanding. My players in Jacksonville used to joke that I was so focused on using every second of every minute of the day that I would plan my restroom breaks a week in advance. Obviously that wasn't true.

A day in advance, maybe.

But on my teams there is very little that is going to happen during the long football season that is spontaneous. We've laid out the path that the team is going to follow. My path, my system. A football team, or in fact any type of organization, is not built to be a democracy. There is no discussion about methods: The team is my responsibility. We design the schedule to accomplish everything we need to get done, and we follow it closely. When my players come to work early in the morning—and I have become well-known in the media for telling players who are only five minutes early for a meeting that they're already late—they know exactly what to expect throughout that day, and at what time to expect it. There are no surprises. We also have a set of rules that every player is expected to follow. The players all know that those rules are going to be enforced equally for every member of the team. The rules are made to provide a predictable framework for the players. At the beginning of the season they are explained clearly, so there won't be any surprises. Those members of our organization who choose not to follow them—that includes everyone, from reserves to stars—will be penalized. No single player on the team is more important than the team. When I speak to the team before a game, I've planned precisely what I'm going to tell them. I don't allow anyone to speak to my team unless I know that the message they will be delivering supports the points we want to emphasize. We don't do anything in preparation that won't lead directly to success.

Everything we do every day, all day, is part of this highly structured, carefully designed system. Every decision we make, every meeting, every practice, is preparation for the game we are going to play on Sunday. None of it is easy. But as a result of all the hard work we've done to prepare, of the dedication we've shown to this system, when my team goes out onto the field on Sunday my players know they have earned the right to win.

When I was the quarterback coach at Boston College I worked with future Heisman Trophy winner Doug Flutie for three seasons. As Doug remembers:

"The years I spent there I was the most disciplined I have ever been in my entire life. In practice [Tom] was tough and meticulous about even the smallest things. For three years he was a voice over my shoulder pointing out the smallest detail. As a result, my biggest fear was making a mental mistake. It was much bigger than making a physical mistake, because it would mean that I hadn't studied long enough or hard enough to do my job. I learned more about football those three years than I did at any other time in my career. Much of my success happened because I knew I was prepared and I was able to relax and perform on game day.

"What I didn't know at the time was how much I learned that carried over into my life off the field. I thought I had a disciplined work ethic and good values when I went to Boston College, but I left there a different person. Everything I had brought with me that mattered had been reinforced, and I also had all the tools I needed to prepare for anything in my life that I wanted to do."

After winning the Heisman his senior year, Doug was a low NFL choice, because scouts believed he was too small and too slow to play quarterback in that league. What they couldn't do was measure the size of his heart. So, after one season in the start-up United States Football League (USFL), he played sporadically in four NFL seasons, then signed with the Canadian Football League. In eight seasons there he led his teams to three Grey Cups (their championship game) and was named the league's outstanding player six different times. Eventually Flutie was named the greatest player in CFL history. After returning to the NFL, he played eight more seasons and was named to the Pro Bowl in 1998. More than that, he brought Boston College to the nation's attention; because of him, applications more than quadrupled.

I had left BC before Doug's senior year, but after seven

years coaching wide receivers with the Eagles, Packers, and Giants, I returned there as head coach in 1991. One day Doug showed up unexpectedly and unannounced at my office. I hadn't seen him or spoken with him in at least six years. I remember this extremely well; I was absolutely delighted to see him. I was very proud of what he had accomplished. So I took one look at him standing in the doorway, a big smile on his face, and after all that time I said warmly, "Hi Doug, when are you getting a haircut?"

We both laughed. While we were now old friends rather than a coach and his player, Doug knew I couldn't let that dig pass.

In addition to developing this system, I am a product of it. As my wife, Judy, will confirm, it doesn't just apply to professional football. In addition to my career, it has been the way I live my life. I believe in it. What is explained in this book is a systematic approach that can be applied to running almost any type of business or achieving any objective. You may have to make certain adjustments, or emphasize different aspects to fit your own situation, but applying this structure will enable you to become the best you can be, and if you do that, winning will follow.

You're reading this book because you hope to apply at least some of this structure to your own life and career and that these changes will make a difference. I believe that they can. It's possible you may win the lottery. Or you may look up one day and find an undrafted free agent who turns out to be Victor Cruz. But you can't depend on that type of good fortune to achieve your goals. The first thing you need to do—always—is clearly define your goal. Whether it's winning the Super Bowl, building a company, or achieving a level of personal success, start by identifying the end. Be as specific as possible: This is where I am going; this is what I intend to accomplish. Once you've done that, you can begin outlining the steps you'll have to take to get there and what you have to do to take each step. Like almost everything else in life, it is a process. The path to success begins with deliberate, determined preparation. Having this structure will help you keep focused, it will provide the confidence you need to keep moving forward, and when you finally get there, it will give you the tremendous satisfaction that you have earned the right to win.

ONE

Build the Structure

A man can be as great as he wants to be. If you believe in yourself and have the courage, the determination, the dedication, the competitive drive, and if you are willing to sacrifice the little things in life and pay the price for the things that are worthwhile, it can be done.

—VINCE LOMBARDI

Normally you begin working toward achieving your objectives from the turf up, but several times in my career we didn't even have turf. At the Rochester Institute of Technology, for example, we had to transform a club football team into a competitive Division III program. We recruited a team by grabbing the biggest kids on campus and convincing them that they really wanted to play football. It was there that this system, which was designed to give players and coaches structure, direction, predictability, and confidence, came into being.

SET A GOAL

In 1995, I became the first head coach of the NFL's expansion Jacksonville Jaguars. I was the seventh person hired by the ownership, and the day I started our entire facility consisted of one trailer stuck in a field of mud. I didn't even have an office; I had a chair at a long folding table. I didn't even have my own telephone; I had to use the owner's phone that was on the table. So I know what it is like to start out from below ground level, from sinking into ankle-deep-mud level. I know what it requires to build a successful organization because I've been part of doing that—several times. The very first thing you have to do is establish a clear goal. Aim high and don't worry about being practical. You don't even have to be realistic; just set a big goal for yourself or your organization. Michelangelo once said, "The greatest danger for most of us is not that we aim too high and we miss; rather our aim is too low and we make it."

Throughout my career in the NFL, everything I've done has been for one purpose: to win the Super Bowl. That's the only goal I've ever been concerned with, but it's exactly the same goal shared by every person in the league: every player, coach, executive, even members of our support staff. That goal is no different in New York than it is in Dallas or Oakland or St. Louis. The real question is, How do you accomplish that? How do you go about winning the Super Bowl?

My basic philosophy has always been simple and direct: Create an environment and provide the direction necessary to allow our players to perform to the best of their ability, which will lead directly to success.

Winning and losing is a measuring stick. That's why we keep score. Winning is an achievement. But getting to that point is the end result of doing the best you can. Winning is what happens when commitment, desire, talent, preparation, hard work, and leadership all come together. There are few things that match the feeling of satisfaction when you know you've done your job to the best of your ability, you've reached a pinnacle, and have been rewarded with victory.

But there are going to be situations in which you do work to the best of your ability and you still don't win. You've put in the time and effort, you've done the work, and you still get beat. Using that measuring stick, you haven't reached your objective, but what you have done is enhanced your chances of winning the next game or the next championship. Creating a structure in which winning is the expectation rather than the hope is a long-term proposition. It takes time and great effort. The first season in Jacksonville, we were in almost every game. We prepared and practiced with the belief that we could win. And we created an environment that made winning possible. The important thing is to continue to make progress, recognize those needs that have to be addressed, and make a plan to do that.

A winning team is a collection of individual players, each one of them fulfilling a clearly defined role, rather than the efforts of one or two great players. Great individual players don't win championships. Teams win championships. The end result has always been far more important than any personal achievement or celebrity. That is the message we have always tried to communicate. We preach team, team, team in everything we do. Team success is our objective: not offense, defense, or special teams. When we win, we all win. I remember how proud I was listening to Michael Strahan in the Giants' locker room after we'd won Super Bowl XLII; he was reminding his teammates, *"I* didn't win the Super Bowl. *You* didn't win the Super Bowl. *We* won the Super Bowl. As a *team!"*

Once you establish a goal you can't take your focus off your objective. Every decision you make should move you toward it, and you have to make a personal commitment to do whatever it takes to accomplish that goal. When I was putting together my staff in Jacksonville, one of the first people I hired was Mike Perkins, who was going to be our video director. At the time, Mike was working in that job at Syracuse University. He came highly recommended by people I trusted. I interviewed him on the phone. When I asked him why he wanted the job in Jacksonville, he told me that at that very moment he was looking out his office window at four feet of snow. I interrupted, telling him, "Look Mike, I wouldn't care if this franchise was in Alaska, you're getting hired here for one reason, and only one reason, and it's not because of the weather. It's for the W. To win." That was the message I delivered the first day and every single day after that, at every opportunity, every way I could, to every person I spoke it. Every decision we made was designed to help us win.

I have never wavered from that. In 2007, the Giants were playing the New England Patriots in the final game of the regular season. New England was 15–0 and trying to complete a perfect season, a historic accomplishment in the NFL. Since 1920 only three teams had gone through the regular season undefeated, and no team had ever been 16–0. The last team with a perfect regular season was the 1972 Miami Dolphins, who finished 14–0 and then won three more post-season games, including the Super Bowl. In terms of play-off position, this game had no meaning. Both teams had already locked in our play-off positions, and the result of the game wasn't going to change a thing. There were many people in the media and a lot of fans who wanted us to keep our best players out of the game, to protect them from injury in preparation for the play-offs. I didn't. While it may have seemed sensible to keep the best players out of the game to prevent them from being hurt, I didn't believe I could preach the gospel of winning and then put out anything less than a complete effort. I'd spent the entire season standing in front of this group of men talking about what it takes to win, what we needed to do to be successful. Then, in the final game of year, against a team on the verge of making history, I was just going to change our lineup and hold key players out of the game? How could I sell that to my team? They would never look at me the same way again. I understood the risks, but giving less than a maximum effort would have contradicted our entire philosophy and compromised our credibility. The essence of competition is giving your best effort.

We did the right thing. If New England was going to set an NFL record, they would have to earn it. We prepared and played that game to win. The fact that we would be playing Tampa Bay in the first round of the play-offs the following week didn't figure in our planning. We went toe-to-toe with New England before losing 38–35. Bill Belichick's team had earned its perfect season; we certainly didn't hand it to them.

After the game John Madden left a message for me on my answering machine that supported our decision. "Just wanted to call and congratulate you and your team on a great effort last night," the message said. "I think it's one of the best things to happen in the NFL in the past ten years. I believe there is only one way to go out and play the game, and that's to win the damn thing. . . . There was so much of the, 'They should rest their players, they don't need to win, therefore they won't win.' That's not what sports is all about, that's not what competition is all about. I'm a little emotional right now, but the NFL needed that, and you guys should be proud."

We were very proud—although it would have been a lot more satisfying if we'd won the game. But it turned out to have been an extremely important game for us. We'd lost the game, but we'd gained a lot. After that we knew we could compete with New England. Many players said, "if this is the best team in the league, we have a real good shot to win it all." Without question, when we played them again several weeks later in the Super Bowl, the confidence we had gained that day certainly contributed to our 17–14 victory.

KNOW WHAT YOU HAVE TO WORK WITH

Every effort has to begin with a realistic appraisal of where you stand.

When I was standing outside our trailer in Jacksonville as the first head coach of the Jaguars, I understood my situation completely: I was sinking into the mud. All I had to do was take a single step up and I had improved my situation. The best place to begin your preparation is to honestly assess the existing situation: How deep in the mud are you? What is the current status of your organization? Who is your competition and how do you compare with them? What do you have to work with? What level of support is available? How much control will you have? How much time? How much money can you spend? What commitments do you have to keep? What hurdles are blocking the way? What is preventing you from winning? You have to be absolutely honest as you assess your standing.

In pro football we begin preparations for our next game by watching tape of our last game. We need to know what we did well and where we failed, because this is exactly what our opponent is assessing, and we need to know what he is seeing. We need to understand where improvement is essential. At the end of every season, we immediately begin preparing for the next season by evaluating our players and our coaching staff. That includes a rigorous critical self-appraisal, a thorough look at what we did right and, more important, where we can make improvements. Before we can begin planning how we're going to get better, we need to honestly and completely assess our strengths and weaknesses. We can't improve without a realistic self-appraisal. The thing you can't do at this point is blame others. Pointing fingers doesn't do anybody any good, and it won't help you get better.

I've walked into several different head coach situations: At both RIT and Jacksonville I was starting the program; I had a blank slate. That was one of the reasons those jobs were so appealing. In both situations my job consisted of being responsible for everything that had to do with touching the football. At RIT that included making the schedule, lining the field, even hiring a cook to prepare team meals. At Jacksonville it ranged from creating the roster to picking out the type of chairs we would use in our meeting rooms.

At Boston College and with the New York Giants I was taking control of losing teams. In those situations you start by figuring out what went wrong under the previous leader, what had prevented them from winning. That's a different type of critical analysis. The obvious answer was that they didn't have enough talent to win, but a lot of times that isn't what happened. When I became the Giants' head coach in 2004, the team was coming off a 4–12 season in which they had lost their final eight games. Although I was actually returning to the Giants (I had been the wide receivers' coach under Bill Parcells from 1988 to 1990, when we won Super Bowl XXV), the organization had changed quite a bit since I had been there. The first thing I did was take a good long look at the situation. That meant determining what had gone wrong, what we had to work with, and how we were going to proceed. It became clear to me quickly that the biggest change that had taken place since I'd been here as a Bill Parcells assistant was a loss of the pride that we had all shared. So, at my first press conference as head coach of the New York Giants, I told the media where we were going to start the rebuilding process. "What we must be about right now," I said, "immediately, is the restoration of pride: self-pride, team pride—the restoration of our professionalism and the dignity with which we conduct our business. We must restore belief in the process by which we will win. We must replace despair with hope and return the energy and passion to New York Giants football." We were going to do that by being firm, fair, honest, and demanding, and by paying close attention to our preparation.

CREATE A STRUCTURE

Where do you begin when starting from scratch? As in any management situation, the first thing we had to do was create an organizational structure that would enable us to build the program. We knew we had to hire a coaching staff, a video staff, and a medical staff, and then begin to build our player roster. We established priorities for each area. In our player development plan, for example, we set positional priorities: quarterback first, then left tackle, right tackle, defensive end . . .

At the same time, we had to create an overall culture that would govern everything we did, a philosophy we would live by that would insure that there was a consistency of purpose and action. A philosophy that allowed us to move forward together. The organizational structure is a reflection of the principles, values, and beliefs of the leader, whether it's the head coach or the CEO. Hall of Fame coach Bill Walsh once said, "The greatest responsibility is to provide for the player an efficient, organized, orderly program of education, of practice and performance." To that I would add that a leader needs to provide consistency. I've worked for several different head coaches, each with their own way of doing things, so I had seen for myself what worked and didn't work. I began my coaching career as a graduate assistant for Ben Schwartzwalder at Syracuse University in 1969, and returned there in 1974 to coach the quarterbacks and offensive backfield under head coach Frank Maloney. Maloney was a disciple of the legendary coaches Bo Schembechler of the University of Michigan and Ohio State's Woody Hayes, both known as strict disciplinarians who ran highly structured programs. So at Syracuse we had pages and pages of details. Each person had a long list of things that he was responsible for: this person had academics, that person had equipment, this person was the only one who could talk to the medical staff. Everything we did every day was detailed. So when something wasn't done, or it went wrong, it was simple to discover the source of the problem and correct it.

At Boston College I was fortunate to work for Jack Bicknell, who surrounded himself with people he trusted and allowed them to coach the way they wanted to. Jack treated his staff like professionals, like men, providing support when they asked for it. He gave his people a lot of responsibility.

I learned from every coach I've worked for—in some

cases that meant what not to do. I believe in a structured program, and that's what I've put in place wherever I've coached. Structured and organized. A program in which everyone knows their responsibilities and that they will be held accountable for the job they were hired to do. It isn't complicated; it's pretty much black and white: This is how things are going to be done, and if you can't do it this way, we're going to find somebody who can.

When we put the first program in place at RIT I told my players, "Consistency, reliability, and determination guarantee progress," and in all the years since then I've never found a reason to change my mind. I've certainly changed many aspects of that program; I've evolved and adapted to keep pace with changes in the game and society, but the foundation on which it's all built has remained firm. To run any type of organization successfully, you've got to have the attention and commitment of everyone you work with. They have to buy in to your program. That begins by providing an overall structure they can depend on not to change. My coaching staff, our players, and the entire support staff know what is expected of them. It's explained very clearly to them that if everyone here is willing to do everything in their power to help us win, we will never have a problem. They can be confident that this structure is going to be the same at the end of the season as it was at the beginning. People need to know what they're going to get every day when they show up for work. The structure is a statement: This is who we are, this is what we do, and this is the way we do it. The principles, values, requirements, and demands of the organization are not going to change. When you come to work tomorrow, nothing will have changed. One of my coaches said about the benefit of consistency, I hope with humor, "If Tom was going to be an ass, he was going to be an ass all the time. We could depend on that."

Once you've set up a strong system with a clear goal, you also have to make a commitment to consistency. You have to stick to it, even when things aren't going right. The road to success has a lot of potholes, and if you changed direction every time you hit one of them, you'd never reach your destination. I brought in Steve Spagnuolo before the 2007 season to be the Giants' defensive coordinator. This was his first job as a defensive coordinator. Steve had been with the Philadelphia Eagles for eight years, coaching their linebackers and defensive backs, and he earned a terrific reputation. When he got to New York he immediately installed an aggressive, blitzing defense that put a lot of pressure on the quarterback. In the first two games that season our defense gave up eighty points. Eighty points! Even our players were wondering if we were doing the right thing. The New York media was ready to hang both Steve and me. They wondered if he was capable of doing the job and blamed me for hiring an inexperienced coordinator. If there was ever a time to think about making some changes, this was it. But we didn't panic. There was no ranting and raving. We had made a commitment to this defensive philosophy, and we weren't going to change the first time it broke down. Or the second. Building a program takes time. We stuck with it, we made some minor adjustments, the players got better at executing their assignments, and in the Super Bowl that year Steve Spagnuolo's defense successfully shut down the highest scoring offense in NFL history, Tom Brady and the New England Patriots.

Admittedly, there are times when it's very hard to stick to your plan. In 2004, my first season as head coach of the New York Giants, General Manager Ernie Accorsi desperately wanted to draft Ole Miss quarterback Eli Manning. This would turn out to be one of the greatest quarterback draft classes in history. In addition to Eli Manning, it included Ben Roethlisberger, Philip Rivers, and Matt Schaub. But Accorsi had scouted Eli when he was playing for the University of Mississippi, and his report began, in all capital letters, "NEVER GETS RATTLED." Eventually he made a deal with San Diego, who had the first pick in the draft; we traded three draft choices, one of them our number four pick, Philip Rivers, to the Chargers for Manning. The Giants' starting quarterback in 2003 had been Kerry Collins, but in the same off-season in which we obtained Manning in the draft, we released Kerry Collins and signed free agent Kurt Warner. Kurt was an experienced veteran who had already won two NFL Most

Valuable Player awards, and he had led the Rams to victory in Super Bowl XXXIV with a record-setting 414 passing yards. In training camp Kurt and Eli competed for the starting job. They went toe-to-toe and, for a rookie, Eli was very impressive. At the end of the camp we decided to go with the veteran Warner as our starting quarterback and give Eli the benefit of learning from him. We started the 2004 season strong, winning five of our first seven games. But then we started playing poorly. After nine games we were still in the play-off mix, with a 5–4 record, but after we lost a game in Arizona that we should have won, I made the decision to make Eli our starting quarterback. We changed quarterbacks; we didn't change our system. In fact, what we were doing was beginning the process of developing our franchise quarterback.

Replacing a proven winner like Kurt Warner with a rookie was not an especially popular decision, and some of our players were very unhappy that we appeared to be sacrificing the season to get Eli Manning the experience he needed for the future. There was a lot of grumbling. As Michael Strahan recalled: "I thought, there go our play-off chances. But the coaches saw something in Eli that we, as players, didn't see right away. We all grew from that experience, and from it I learned to trust them. There's a reason they are in those coaching positions." But at that time it didn't help the situation when Eli got off to a terrible start. In his first four games we scored only thirty-seven points.

There was no doubt that Kurt Warner was still a great football player. After that season he became a free agent and played five more seasons, with the Arizona Cardinals, leading them to the Super Bowl in 2008. But I believed at that time that Eli Manning was the future of the New York Giants, and it was time to start the process. Once I'd made that decision, I never wavered. While I didn't read the newspapers, I certainly was aware of the criticism about my decision. It would have been impossible not to be. But once I had made it, unless something drastic happened there was no way I was going to change it. We had set our goal, we'd assessed the situation, and we'd built a system. Making it work required a commitment to stay the course. I wasn't going to start changing the way we did things when it didn't work right away or when the media criticized me. This was as much about the type of team culture we were building in New York as it was about winning those football games.

It got bad. In early December we played Washington and then Baltimore, two very good defensive teams. Every team is going to bring as much pressure as possible against a rookie quarterback. They're going to try to shake him. They attacked Eli on every play, and they never stopped coming after him. He didn't handle it very well. He had a 0.0 quarterback rating at the end of the half against the Baltimore Ravens. I didn't want to destroy his confidence, so I put Kurt Warner back in for the second half. But Eli remained our starting quarter-back. We lost seven consecutive games that season, dropping our record to 5–10. This was Eli's initiation into the NFL. He had to learn and fight his way through it. There were no shortcuts.

The Monday morning after that Baltimore game Eli came into my office to talk about it. He told me he was worried that we might be thinking about doing something differ-ently. He knew he hadn't been productive, but he wanted to reassure me that I hadn't made a mistake, that he was going to get better. He was pretty emotional.

I told him that he was our guy, period. I explained that teams were going to continue to come after him until he proved he could handle it. Then I reiterated to the team that Eli Manning was our quarterback, and that we were going to win with him. The following week we played a solid game against the Steelers, who were led by rookie Ben Roethlis-berger to a 15–1 regular season record. Although we lost that game, we did beat the Cowboys in the final game of the sea-son: Dallas scored with 1:49 left in the game, to take a 24–21 lead, but Eli drove the team sixty-three yards in five plays to put us on the Dallas three-yard line with eleven seconds left and no time-outs. We gave Eli a built-in pass/run audible. If you run and don't make it, you lose the game; there is not enough time to get lined up and spike the ball. But at the line of scrimmage Eli saw that the Cowboys safeties were playing back in pass coverage and alerted to the audible. It was a gutsy call with the game on the line, and it worked—Tiki Barber ran the ball in for the touchdown. That was an important win for us, because it set a positive tone for the off-season. It was a real sign of progress. Eli had weathered the storms of his rookie year to have enough confidence to make the correct call. It left us with hope and excitement about the future.

The structure that would eventually lead to success was in place. We hadn't won, but we had established the parameters that would enable us to become the best team we could be. The first step was done.

ESTABLISH THE RULES AND ENFORCE THEM

The culture of an organization is defined by its rules. The rules are used to set the tone and the expectations. I have earned a reputation for running a very tough organization. Very tough, very tight. I believe in establishing a set of rules and following them; that has never changed. But what has changed are the rules themselves. Rules have to be sensible, realistic, and timely. The purpose of setting rules is not to harass your people but rather to establish and maintain discipline. When you're managing a large group of people, there have to be guidelines. The discipline you follow off the field will lead to success on the field. Placekicker Lawrence Tynes explained our philosophy when he pointed out, "[Coughlin] wants us to be perfect. He wants us to be the best dressed team on game day. He wants us to be the most organized, and he wants us to be like that in practice. Every kick has to be made, every punt has to be long and out of bounds or on the sideline, and every snap has to be perfect."

Rules are like the traffic lights of real life: If you don't have a set of rules by which everyone abides, you have chaos, and when you have chaos, there is no structure, and you lose. Whatever rules you make, they have to be stated clearly, so there are no gray areas. Everything needs to be spelled out, with no room for interpretation. In the NFL's collective bargaining agreement the league's ownership and the NFL Players Association have laid the groundwork for what a team can and cannot do. The rules cover everything from the number of practice sessions we can have to the amount of money, per pound, we can fine players. Every team has to follow those rules. But, in addition, we have established our own team rules.

Beyond simply setting a code of conduct and instructing people about what is permitted or prohibited, those rules have other purposes. They are designed to bring the team together, create a professional environment in which we can get all our work done with a minimum of distraction, and help develop pride in the organization. In the first few years in Jacksonville, for example, setting and enforcing a strict set of rules helped a large group of individuals bond together over a common theme—hating me. It was the one thing on which they could all agree.

Setting tough rules is also a good way of finding out quickly who is committed to the program and who isn't, who's going to buy into our philosophy and be willing to pay the price and who wants out, who is in the trenches with us when it gets tough and who isn't. The purpose of setting rules isn't to catch people and punish them but rather to find those people who are willing to make a commitment to the team and their teammates.

No team or large organization is automatically a big happy family. You've got a lot of individuals with different needs and desires and talent levels, and the rules level the ground for all of them. In the past, my teams have griped about my rules. There were always players who believed the rules I set weren't always fair or were too petty. I agreed that they had a right to their opinions—as long as they followed all the rules that I believed were necessary to prepare, practice, and play at a championship level. I didn't think putting on a tie when we traveled, for example, was too much to demand.

I still feel that way about following the rules, but the actual rules may be different. They've evolved. At one time I wouldn't allow my coaches to wear sunglasses in practice, for example, because I wanted them to be able to look players right in the eyes. That was my idiosyncrasy, and I understood that, but I still enforced it. No more. Certain people may even need to wear sunglasses for health reasons. So that rule doesn't exist anymore.

Nowadays, I have fewer rules, too. Tony Boselli, an offensive lineman who was our first pick in the history of the franchise at Jacksonville and who eventually became the cornerstone of our success, used to complain that he needed to carry a cheat sheet just to keep all of our rules straight. That certainly wouldn't be true anymore.

But then and now, every rule I set has a purpose. Be on time every time. Know your assignments on the field. Conduct yourself like a professional on and off the field. Demonstrate pride in our organization. Respect your teammates. Pay complete attention in our meetings.

The most important team rule has always been "be on time." That has always been the golden rule for me. If you're on time, most everything else will fall into place. Be where you're supposed to be when you're supposed to be there, prepared to go to work.

It's been my experience that people actually want discipline. They like structure, as long as it is explained completely and enforced uniformly. At Jacksonville, we had a very young team, and the rules that I enforced encouraged professional behavior. My intention was to build pride in the organization. I wanted my players to understand that playing for the Jacksonville Jaguars in the National Football League was a privilege, and that sometimes it meant surrendering your individuality.

When I set the rules I always felt it was better to start out with a firm set, and then, if the situation warranted it, make the necessary adjustments. Michael Strahan summed it up accurately: "If you come in easy on your employees or your teammates and then try to become a hard man, it doesn't work. But to come in and establish your rules, tell people what you expect, and then give them some leeway, do it that way and people will respect you. As a manager of any kind it's easier to be a tough guy and then show a little softer side, because once you show that soft side, it's very hard to come back and be tough."

Most of my rules came from my own experiences. I kept notes at every level of my career and learned what rules worked for me and what I would do differently. Both as a player and an assistant coach I saw which rules effectively allowed me to accomplish my objectives and which ones caused more problems than they were worth. Not every rule is equally important. Through the years I learned which were important and which made less of a difference. Then I enforced those things that were important. While many of my players may not have liked it, eventually they all came to understand that following them was a basic requirement of earning the right to win.

As a leader, your credibility depends completely on the way you enforce the rules you've made. For them to have any value, they have to apply equally to everyone.

I was fortunate to spend an afternoon with UCLA's famed basketball coach John Wooden near the end of his life. This is a man I had long admired and at least in some ways modeled myself after. Wooden also strictly enforced his rules. I asked him about a much publicized example of his discipline, and he acknowledged that it was true. Coach Wooden did not permit his players to have facial hair. That was a team rule. Once, when the team began practice at the beginning of the season, his All-American center Bill Walton showed up with a beard. Wooden called him over and asked pleasantly, "Bill, have you forgotten something?"

Bill Walton, apparently ready for this confrontation, responded, "Coach, if you mean the beard, I think I should be allowed to wear it. It's my right."

"Do you believe in that strongly?" John Wooden asked him.

"Yes I do, Coach. Very much."

Wooden continued, "Bill, I have great respect for individuals who stand up for those things in which they believe. I really do. And the team is going to miss you."

Walton realized that Wooden was serious, that no individual was more important than the team. He went inside the locker room and returned minutes later, clean shaven. As Wooden added, after telling that story, "He understood the choice was between his own desires and the good of the team, and Bill was a team player. I think if I had given in to him I would have lost control not only of Bill but of his teammates."

My experience has been that John Wooden was correct. The day you don't enforce your rules you might as well just do away with them. Your credibility is at stake if you don't enforce them. Some rules may be made to be broken, but not mine. When you don't enforce your rules, people begin losing respect for you. In our very first minicamp at Jacksonville a veteran free agent lineman we'd brought in as a potential starter got into a fight with another player. Fights happen in practice; it isn't that unusual. Football is a gladiator sport. But we don't like fighting, and we certainly don't encourage it. The risk of injury is part of the game, and fighting is an unnecessary addition to that risk. But when two players fight, we break it up and go on with practice. After this fight ended I told one player to pick up his helmet and go over to the sidelines. He picked his helmet and threw it thirty yards in the air. We escorted him from the practice field. His behavior was a direct challenge, but it was also an opportunity to make my point. I called the team together, told them that there was one person in charge, and whether they liked it or not, things were going to be done my way. The next day I released the player who had challenged the rules. Point made.

In December 2011, the night before we played at Dallas in a game we had to win to have any chance of making the play-offs, Ahmad Bradshaw, our leading rusher, missed curfew. At that time the team was struggling; we'd lost our previous four games, and several New York sportswriters were predicting I would be fired if we missed the play-offs. There was no question that the team was stronger with Ahmad Bradshaw in our lineup. But by breaking a basic rule he had violated every principle I believe in. I either had to prostitute my values to the idea of winning at all costs and make an exception in this situation, or enforce the rule. What was the cost to my team, and to me, of enforcing the rule? And was I willing to pay that price? It was not a pleasant situation to be in, but I'd been there, or close to it, several times before.

That certainly wasn't the first time I'd had to bench a player for breaking team rules. Ahmad Bradshaw knew the rules and had seen me enforce them. But the stakes had never been this high before. Our opportunity to make the play-offs, and possibly my job, were on the line. The first thing I did was confirm that the information I had received was correct. It was. After that, I don't think anyone who was part of our program had any doubt about what I was going to do. The only question was, What would Bradshaw's punishment be? To begin with, he knew he was going to be fined. That hurt him where he didn't want to be hurt. I also knew that Bradshaw took great pride in the fact that he was starting for the New York Giants. So I decided to bench him for the entire first half.

I felt I didn't have a choice. If you are in a leadership position in any organization, in any job, and you compromise your principles the first time you face adversity, you'll lose all your credibility. After you compromise once, who is going to believe you the next time? The entire structure suddenly becomes shaky. Your word has lost its value. It was not difficult for me to make this decision. What was hard for me to understand was, Why would someone risk being forced to miss the game? Once again, earning the right to win means making a difficult or even unpopular decision and sticking to it. The principles and values that form the cornerstone of our beliefs cannot be compromised.

While I'm certain many people privately questioned my decision, to their credit the entire organization, our ownership, the front office, and the players all publicly supported me. And Bradshaw took his punishment without complaint. He understood the situation and my decision. Instead of sitting on the bench and pouting, he enthusiastically cheered his teammates from the sideline. Bradshaw did play in the second half, gaining 12 yards on eight carries. Brandon Jacobs had his best game of the season, carrying the ball 19 times for 101 yards. It was a very close game, and our players stepped up. Fortunately, defensive end Jason Pierre-Paul blocked a last-second field goal attempt from the 47-yard line, and we won, 37–34. Few things in life are sweeter than sticking to your principles in the face of adversity and emerging victorious.

BE RESILIENT

I have always believed that people want to work in an environment that is structured, disciplined, and consistent. In this system, workers know exactly what is expected. Sticking to your structure makes it easier to deal with surprises, setbacks, and obstacles. There will be times when we all have to overcome adversity—but we believe adversity makes us stronger. Things are going to go wrong in life, and the best laid plans will go astray. In my business the unexpected happens every day. How you overcome those obstacles will go a long way toward determining whether or not you'll be successful. Having an established system that people can rely on makes it a lot easier to keep them from losing focus, becoming anxious, being depressed, even panicking when something goes wrong. We don't want our players getting too high or too low. They accept the reality that setbacks are part of the business and that the people in charge—the coaching staff—knows how to deal with it.

Unlike most other businesses, we know we are going to

lose several players to injury during the season. Professional football isn't like an insurance company, in which people can work when hurt and still be effective. In pro football, every team has to be prepared to have substitutes to step in when the situation arises without having to make drastic changes to the rest of their system. Your success in doing that will always have a substantial impact on the season. We work with the Giants' general manager, Jerry Reese, to create the depth of talent we know we're going to need, but once Jerry brings in those people, it's the responsibility of the coaching staff to insure that they are prepared to contribute if the opportunity arises. At the beginning of the 2011 season, for example, it seemed like we were losing an important player every day. Our middle linebacker smacked his knee and went down; our starting corner and his backup each tore a ligament and were lost for the season. A defensive end we were depending on had arthroscopic surgery on his knee. Our other defensive end injured his neck. I'd never seen anything like it. Before the season started we had already lost five players for the season. Both our first and second round draft picks were injured. Physically, the team was devastated. My job was to just keep moving forward. Regardless of what I thought or did when I went into my office, shut the door, and pulled down the shades, when I stood in front of the team I had to reinforce the fact that we were prepared for this.

The first thing I always do is acknowledge the injured

player. I make sure that everybody knows we feel terrible for that player. Every person in that room knows how difficult it is to play in the NFL and is aware how quickly and easily a career can end. Players live with the knowledge that they are always one play away from the end of their career. Then, having acknowledged the player, who's next? Next man up, we call it. Let's get on with it. That injury means someone is going to get a tremendous opportunity to prove the type of player he is, because as a team we are only as strong as the fifty-third player on our roster. The player moving up is part of the same system. If he has done his job, he has been preparing for this challenge his entire career. His daily routine will barely change. If we've done our job, we have prepared our people to step up into that spot when they are needed. Early in the 2012 season, for example, the team was hit very hard by injuries. We lost four key starting players before our mid-September game with the Carolina Panthers: running back Ahmad Bradshaw, receivers Hakeem Nicks and Domenik Hixon, and right tackle David Diehl. We were depending on our reserves to step up. Both running back Andre Brown, who had been cut seven times by five different teams, including the Giants, in the previous three years, and receiver Ramses Barden, who had a total of fifteen receptions in three NFL seasons, were well prepared. They had been waiting a long time for this opportunity and knew exactly what we expected from them. Brown carried twenty times for 113 yards and two touchdowns, while Barden had nine receptions for 138 yards, leading us to a 36–7 win. "I'm proud of the guys," Eli Manning said after the game. "At this level, in this league, you never know when you're going to get an opportunity. You have to be prepared for it, and you have to step up. A lot of guys have come in and done that."

"We know how good these guys are," Victor Cruz added. "We see it every day in practice."

The ability to substitute for an injured player without losing too much at that position will go a long way in determining the outcome of the game, and maybe even the entire season. We know our opponent is going to test that substitute over and over until he proves he can do the job. We know that's true because we do the same thing. This is why we emphasize the concept that a team is only as strong as its fifty-third player. The other players understand the situation and provide as much help as possible—but we don't make substantial changes. We expect our reserves to prepare as if they are going to play every week. We give them the same tools we give our starters. So when we are hit by a rash of injuries, nobody panics; we know we've put in the time preparing for this situation. The result is as smooth a transition as possible. And in 2011, we were able to overcome those injuries and win the Super Bowl.

It is a waste of time feeling sorry for ourselves; other teams face the same problem, so we never use an injury as an excuse. We just go back to work, doing the same things the same way we have always done them. It may not make up for the loss of a starting player, but at least it mitigates the impact on the whole team. And believe me, if you manage to overcome that many obstacles to your goal, you have earned the right to win.

BUILD AN ORGANIZATION WITH CHARACTER

The sage Andy Rooney said, "I've learned that the easiest way to grow as a person is to surround myself with people smarter than I am." Fortunately, I've done pretty well by following this advice.

Our type of highly structured system isn't a good fit for everyone; there are people whose personalities just aren't right for this type of environment. They simply need more flexibility, more individual freedom. The key to building a system that functions smoothly is to find people who share your vision, hire them, and allow them to do their job. Nothing will be more important to the success of your organization than the people you hire to implement your philosophy. It's a pretty simple formula: Organizations are devised of people, therefore, the greater the quality of the people, the greater the organization will be. This is true for any type of organization, and it includes people on every level: executives, management, and support staff. Every employee matters. A single message that doesn't get delivered can cause serious problems. The question is, what characteristics do you look for when you're bringing people into your organization?

My personality is not a well-kept secret: I can be tough, I can be demanding, and there is a rumor that I have a temper. In fact, my wife, Judy, claims that when we're in the car I will get into an argument with the GPS, second-guessing its directions: "A right turn here? That can't be right. Are you sure?" But I believe I'm also fair, supportive, and very loyal to the people who do their job. I seek out and appreciate people with those same values.

I've done a good deal of hiring on all levels in my career, from a cook to prepare team meals at RIT to offensive and defensive coordinators in the NFL. Whenever I've built an organization I've made it a point to surround myself with people who share my competitive spirit and who will sacrifice and do all the little things that will put us in a position to earn the right to win. Egos must be controlled. *The success of the program will rise or fall on the ability, initiative, imagination, and determination of the members of our staff.* When we built the Jacksonville organization, for example, I was responsible for hiring every person involved with the football program. So I do know how difficult it can be to find the right person to fill your need. When I am hiring someone, I try to remember the wise advice of George Washington: "Associate yourself with men of good quality if you esteem your own reputation; for 'tis better to be alone than in bad company."

The first thing we look for is ability. The person has to be able to do the job, whether it's preparing breakfast for 110 people, sacking a quarterback, or tracking a lost package. Once we establish that they are capable, we look to see if they are a certain type of person. Once again, I agree completely with John Wooden, who advised, "Have the courage to make character count among the qualities you seek in others." While each situation is different, there are certain common themes about the hiring process: Whether I am hiring support staff, assistant coaches, or even players, in every interview I look for and talk about the great all-American work ethic, the ability of an individual to recognize the demands of the job and the willingness to go beyond that. I want to know if this person is a self-starter; do they have the pride to do more than simply get the job done? A character-based, value-centered philosophy has always been the backbone of my organization.

I also look for intangibles, such as commitment and enthusiasm. At Jacksonville I wanted players who were willing to relocate to the area and live there year-round. For me that would prove that they were willing to make a real commitment to the Jaguars organization. In addition to establishing a rapport and team spirit, being near our facility in the off-season would benefit a player's physical preparation. When teammates work out together they compete; they want to lift more weights, run faster, do more reps. The NFL's collective bargaining agreement made off-season programs completely voluntary, so I had to make it clear that I was looking for volunteers for these workouts. But I knew that if they weren't willing to make that all-in commitment to the team and their teammates in the off-season, they probably wouldn't fit into the type of program I was trying to build. As Jeff Lageman, one of the first free agents we signed, remembered, "If you wanted to play for Jacksonville, you were going to be there in the off-season. No bones about it."

Position coaches and coordinators, like department managers in a business organization, will be the team's authority figures. They will spend more time with the players than the head coach. They can either support the head coach or, as most coaches have seen at least once in their career, sabotage him. That's why it's so important to put together a staff of people with great character. People you respect, like, and trust. Most of the coaches I've hired I had worked with previously on other coaching staffs or had gotten a strong recommendation about from people I trust. They're coaches who have a proven record. Coaching may be a wonderful career, but it's a difficult life. Almost without exception, every successful coach has been fired at some time in his career. It may not have been his fault, he may have done a terrific job, but football is a team game, and when a head coach is replaced, his entire staff often goes with him. Conversely, coaches may also be leaving for different jobs, moving up the coaching ladder to jobs that give them more responsibility or pay better, or simply to more desirable programs. As a result there is always a lot of movement throughout the profession, and during a long career you'll end up working with numerous people. Over the years coaches earn a reputation: he's a hard worker, he coaches the 3–4 defense, his players love him. You get to know those people you want to work with. I've always kept a list of college coaches looking to move up as well as coaches in professional football that I'd be interested in interviewing to fill a particular vacancy.

When I began looking for a defensive coordinator to help me build the program at Jacksonville in 1995, for example, one of the first people I contacted was Dick Jauron. We had worked together on Forrest Gregg's staff at Green Bay; I coached wide receivers and Dick coached the defensive secondary. My offensive players competed with his defensive players on the field and in drills so we had gotten to know each other. I respected his knowledge of the game, his ability to relate to his players, and his work ethic. I knew from my own experience that Dick Jauron had the type of character I wanted as part of my organization. But still, as I did with everyone I was interested in hiring, I conducted a long interview with him. I already knew about his character and his values. Dick is the salt of the earth. So we talked about his coaching philosophy, how he would run his defense, what he thought about certain players. Mostly, though, we established a comfort zone with each other.

When you're building your roster you often have to bring in players you don't know much about. In those situations, the interviewing process was really important for me. When we were preparing for our first draft in Jacksonville we were considering taking offensive lineman Tony Boselli with our first pick. The first pick in franchise history is a big deal. The first pick was going to be a building block. So in addition to looking at hours of film and putting him through the skills tests, I took Boselli and his then fiancée and now wife, Angie, out to dinner. During that dinner I asked both Tony and Angie probing questions about his life away from football. I asked him about his dreams for his future, what interested him, how he spent his free time. We knew he had talent, that was obvious from watching him play, but we didn't know the quality of his character. But by the day of the draft we knew the person as well as the player we were getting when we selected him. He told me after the draft that I was the only coach to get to know him on that level off the field.

Character is essential. Essential. Believe me, when you are going to be working closely with someone for a long time, character counts. We have always looked for people who are willing to do whatever is necessary to help the whole organization succeed, rather than being motivated by personal achievement. In our system "we" always supersedes "me." That isn't always easy in the NFL, where uniquely talented people are being paid huge salaries and are treated like celebrities. That's one reason I insist that the same rules apply to every player and that no one is given special treatment. But people with good character never act, speak, or infer that they expect or deserve special treatment. In fact, it's quite the opposite.

No matter what profession you're talking about, whether it's professional sports or a nine-to-five office situation, almost inevitably there are going to be situations in which character will make a significant difference. When you're dealing with adversity or you have to sacrifice personal achievement for the good of the team or you aren't getting the opportunity you think you've earned, you need to have a personal reservoir of character to draw on. As a coach or a manager, you want to work with dedicated people who have values similar to your own, people you can depend on to be there when things get tough. The more of those good character people you have in key positions the better chance you have to succeed.

Character also accelerates the growth of talent. In 2010, we were considering using our first-round pick to draft a young Haitian who had grown up in Florida named Jason Pierre-Paul. It was obvious he had a great deal of natural talent, but there were some warning signs in his record: He had bounced around schools and hadn't played a lot of major college football. But General Manager Jerry Reese insisted we get to know him on a personal level and therefore deserves all the credit for Jason becoming a New York Giant. When we sat down and spoke with him, it very quickly became obvious that he was a good kid. He had grown up in a bilingual home, where both English and Creole were spoken, and he hadn't had the academic opportunities other kids had had. We began to find out some things about his character: He was caring for his blind father and helping to raise his younger sisters. The fact that he didn't have as much playing experience as we would have liked didn't bother us. Anyone could see he had raw talent, so his upside was exciting. And once we got to know him, Jerry was confident that if we brought him into our program and surrounded him with good people, he would become an asset. The support system he would need was already in place, and after learning about his character we were confident he could be molded into a great player in our environment. Since we drafted him Jason has worked hard to improve, and he has become an impact player for us. At the end of the 2011 season he earned first team All-Pro honors and was named to the Pro Bowl. But most impressive is that even after he has played a very good game, rather than being satisfied, the first thing he does is look to see what mistakes he made and what he can do to get better.

Conversely, there have been many talented young football players who we knew after a single interview didn't fit our program. The most important question I ask myself when conducting an interview is, Do I really want to introduce this individual into our team culture? What's the fit? If they have a red mark on their record, a problem with a coach, or they were caught smoking marijuana, we talk about it with them. In some cases there is a lot more to the story, or it truly was a one-time event, but usually we can tell when the answers are too pat, when some smart agent has prepared his client for these questions. There have been numerous instances when Jerry Reese and I looked at each other after a kid has walked out of the interview room and we don't even have to discuss it. We both know that player didn't have a clue about what it would take to succeed in our organization. Not everybody we've brought in has worked out. I've made mistakes. When that happens we've tried to rectify the situation as quickly as possible. I don't show a lot of patience with people who are not willing to make a total commitment to the team or who demonstrate a lack of self-discipline. This is true for everyone from the equipment manager to a starting player. We find the complainers and the whiners, the people who aren't willing to put in the long hours, the people more interested in self-promotion than the success of the team and get rid of them as quickly as possible. When we identify a person with a bad attitude or a questionable work ethic, or an individual who can't buy into the team concept, then we are going to make a change. I've often paraphrased Abraham Lincoln: A team divided is not going to be victorious. Your success as a team is going to be greatly hampered by someone who, by virtue of his attitude, is not willing to do what is necessary for the good of the team. Unfortunately, at times the malcontents are very, very productive players. In that situation you do your best to win them over, to make them understand what you're trying to do and get them to buy into it. But when it becomes necessary, the only thing you can do is admit that they don't fit in the program and get rid of them. No matter how talented a player may be, you can't ignore a lack of character or pretend it isn't going to affect your entire program.

Sometimes you just need to get rid of a bad apple. Cutting those people really will cut your losses. Anyone who is serious about building a long-term program has had to do this. Several times we've had to release a productive player and replace him in our lineup with a less talented player, and almost always I've found that over a season or two it makes little, if any, difference. The system has been built to allow someone to step up and take advantage of the opportunity. That's what happened in Jacksonville in 1994, when wide receiver Jimmy Smith, who had been released by both the Cowboys and the Eagles, got the opportunity to move into the starting lineup when we released a free agent Pro Bowl receiver we'd signed in the middle of the season. The player we released had actually come into work one morning hungover, his hat pulled down low over his eyes. He was honest about it, admitting he had been out late drinking the night before. Hungover on a Friday morning during the season? Amazing. That veteran still had great talent, but it was obvious we could no longer trust his character. He was putting his own desires way in front of the team's. He didn't fit. After we released him he quickly signed with another team. He went on to play on a Super Bowl–winning team and made another Pro Bowl. But he didn't fit into our program. Given the opportunity, Jimmy Smith took his position and became a star. By the time he retired he was the seventh-leading receiver in NFL history, he had been selected for five Pro Bowls, and accounted for more than 12,000 yards. Getting rid of a problematic person may hurt the program for a brief period of time, in our case for a game or two. But I guarantee that the long-term gain is eventually far more important than the short-term loss. No one is irreplaceable.

DELEGATE AUTHORITY

One of the most difficult things for me to learn was how to delegate authority. Early in my head-coaching career I insisted on taking charge of everything, from the color of the paint on the locker room walls to calling the plays we would run. Gradually I learned that it was impossible to manage that much and do it all well. There was too much for one person to do, so I put people I trusted in positions and gave them specific responsibilities—although I still asked them to run most things by me. Eventually, though, as people proved themselves, I got out of their way as much as I am capable of doing and let them do their jobs. That is still not easy for me, it's just not my nature, but it is absolutely necessary. A successful coach or manager delegates responsibility and allows people he trusts to do their jobs.

Once the right people are in the right places, you have to trust them to do their jobs in a timely fashion, and to do them right. Usually, rather than dictating a decision, what I'll do is ask a lot of questions then make suggestions. I try not to impose my will. I may not agree with their decision, but I trust them. I know that they've spent every minute of their workweek preparing to make that decision, so sometimes I just have to bite my tongue and let them make it. I know it's not always going to be perfect. But when it does succeed I'll be the first person to congratulate them.

But I never forget that in the end I am ultimately responsible for the success or the failure of the organization. It's on me. I tell my coaches that I am going to do whatever it requires for this program to succeed. There's no room for any lack of effort or loyalty. If I want something done a certain way, that's my prerogative. When we have discussions, I want to hear their opinions. I'll listen to them and consider them—but once I make a decision as to a course of action, I expect everyone to support that decision.

Hire people you trust, clearly delineate their responsibilities, communicate with them regularly and clearly so they understand your intention, offer them help when they need it, give them support when it's necessary, and then leave them alone to do the job you hired them to do. When Steve Spagnuolo's defense gave up eighty points in our first two games in 2007 I asked him to meet me in the office at 6:00 A.M. on Friday morning. We spent forty-five minutes reviewing tapes of our practices during the week. In that meeting I asked him a lot of questions: Why are we doing it this way? Would it make a difference if we did it that way? Are you ready if the Redskins run this on Sunday? How are we going to handle that? Are you sure you want to do it that way? I never criticized him, but I did challenge him. I made some suggestions, but I never tried to dictate what he should do. I had hired him because of what he had done over the previous eight years. I could also judge him on the two weeks' work I'd seen him do, and I believed he was doing a good job even if the results weren't what we desired at that point. If I didn't think he knew what he was doing, I shouldn't have hired him. Instead I tried to be supportive and to help him with his preparation. We began meeting regularly every Friday morning.

At first, as Steve has admitted, he thought these sessions were a pain in the neck and fought them a little bit. He had a lot of work to do and I was keeping him from doing it. But by the fifth or sixth week, he told me, he had started looking forward to our sessions. They forced him to focus just a little more directly on what we intended to do. In addition to the preparation we did, the subtext of those meetings was that I had complete confidence in him and his staff. I trusted him.

Our third game was the turning point of the 2007 season. We were trailing Washington 17–3 at the half. In the second half our defense finally kicked in. Everything we'd been preaching started working. We held them scoreless and took a 24–17 lead. But with fifty-eight seconds left in the game, the Redskins had a first and goal at our 1-yard line. They had no time-outs left and were going without a huddle. One yard, that's all they needed. We stopped them on the first three downs. One play for the game. I could see our linemen were winded, and I thought maybe we should take a time-out to give them a breather. I asked Steve if he wanted me to call time so we could get the right defensive call in. He was decisive. No, he said. Washington's offense looked like they were having trouble getting organized, and he didn't want to give them any additional time. Instead, he signaled for the same defensive alignment we'd just run.

If I had been calling defensive signals, it's possible I would have taken that time-out. But if I really wanted him to run our defense, then I had to let him make that call. I either trusted him to make key decisions or I didn't. My commitment to him was on the goal line too. It was his call, and I let him make it, and it turned out to be the right one. We stuffed them for no gain and ran off the field with our first win of the season. In addition to rebuilding confidence in our defense, that one series of downs helped solidify my relationship with my defensive coordinator.

The foundation of winning is the structure you build, the culture you instill, and the people you work with every day. Once an organization is in place and functioning, meaning everyone from the receptionist to the quarterback is contributing by doing his or her job to the best of their ability, you are free to focus on those aspects that will make you better, from the way you fill every minute of the day, the week, the month, and the year to the way you motivate other people to bring their best game.

TWO

The Time of Your Life: Scheduling

Determine never to be idle. No person will have occasion to complain of the want of time who never loses any. It is wonderful how much can be done if we are always doing.

—THOMAS JEFFERSON

Time is the blank canvas of preparation. You earn the right to win by using your time more productively and effectively than your competition. Every one of us has the same 60 minutes every hour, 168 hours every week, 52 weeks every year to fill. How you choose to fill that time will be the difference between success and failure.

USE TIME EFFECTIVELY

I'm both a long-term and short-term planner. I make a schedule for the future, I map out the hours in a day, and I break down the minutes in the hour. I usually begin by making a list, sometimes on paper, sometimes in my head, of everything I need to get done during the day. Then I block out the day, the week, the month, and the year to make certain I get it all accomplished.

I try to expand the day as much as possible. Most head coaches know that during the season you may end up spending some nights sleeping in the office. In this profession, working long hours is a given, but just putting in the time isn't enough. There are no trophies awarded for working the most hours. It isn't how much time you spend working, it's what you accomplish during that time. Activity shouldn't be mistaken for achievement. The goal is to make the most effective use of your time.

Since it's impossible to create any more hours, I'll try to get more done in the time available by squeezing waste out of my schedule. I don't like to waste a second. Literally, a second. When we were building our facility in Jacksonville we had two sets of locker rooms off the field. The locker rooms at the entrance to the tunnel were built to be used for college games. The Jaguars' locker room was at the far end of the tunnel, maybe an additional forty-five steps. While the stadium was under construction I had an assistant go onto the field with a stopwatch and determine how much longer it would take to get from the sideline to our locker room than to get to the college locker room. I wondered if we could gain any time by using the college locker room at halftime. It wasn't enough time to make a difference, but it was important to know in order to make a decision.

Anybody who has worked with me will agree that I am obsessed with the effective use of time. Being on time has to be a priority. If it isn't, then the job is not their priority at that point. Something else is more important. People who know me sometimes joke that I'm going to show up early for my own funeral. Our program follows what people on the staff refer to as "Coughlin Time." Generally, Coughlin Time is five minutes earlier than the actual time. Every clock in our facility that the players have to deal with is set five minutes fast. Real time 9:55 A.M. is 10 A.M. Coughlin Time in our facility. Even then, when we have a meeting scheduled, my players understand that if they are not there five minutes early, they are already late. Everybody laughs at that until they're the one who's only two minutes early and they can't get into the meeting room. Or they come down from their hotel room at real time to get the team bus to the stadium only to discover it was operating on Coughlin Time. I think people began to understand I was serious about this during my first season in New York. We were on the road and future Hall of Fame defensive end Michael Strahan came downstairs at only a few minutes before the real time the bus was scheduled to leave— and discovered it had already left. Michael was one of the leaders of the team. When people realize you're willing to leave a great player like Michael Strahan behind, I guarantee that they will start paying real close attention to the clock.

I started operating this way at RIT and I haven't really changed. If you're not early, you're late. Coughlin Time generally applies to anything in the organization directly related to the team. So when someone from the football side is scheduled to meet with someone from the operations side, an accountant for example, one of them will invariably ask, "Is that real time or Coughlin Time?" My primary reason for operating like this is that I want people to come to work early and hungry and prepared. This is your job; there might be eighty thousand people cheering for you on Sunday, but it is still a job for which you are being paid. If you can't be ready to go on Coughlin Time, then it seems to me you aren't completely committed to the process. And I make it very clear that there will be penalties for being late. My first year with the Giants there was a lot of resistance to this way of operating. People complained pretty loudly about it, but by the middle of the season everybody was in the meeting room ready to go to work at least five minutes before we were scheduled to start. They began to understand the concept of Coughlin Time. This is another means of weeding out those people who are not committed to improvement, to winning. Once you start functioning like this, it becomes habitual. Whatever it takes, you'll find yourself showing up early and prepared to go to work.

MAKE A SCHEDULE AND FOLLOW IT

Let me repeat that: Make a schedule and follow it. It's that important. We make schedules to insure that everybody is on the same page. We make long-term schedules, medium-term schedules, and daily schedules. And then we follow them. Doing that means that our players can rely on the fact that we will be doing exactly what is on the schedule when it is scheduled to be done.

We operate efficiently; we don't waste time. We even make optional schedules so we are prepared for different scenarios. When the league and the Players Association were fighting over the collective bargaining agreement in 2011, the players were locked out of their stadiums and facilities from the beginning of April to the end of July. That meant we couldn't practice; we couldn't do anything. Coaching assistant Chris Pridy drew up our potential off-season schedule at the beginning of the lockout, and then he updated it every single day, so if the lockout suddenly ended the very next day, we were ready to go to work without losing any time. Obviously, for several months we knew that the situation wasn't close to being resolved but that didn't matter; we still drew up a new schedule every day and remained prepared to get right to work.

In training camp, we even make different practice schedules in case the weather changes: If it rains or if rain is forecasted, we will adjust our starting time and practice location.

There are days for which we will have three completely different practice schedules depending on the forecast.

During the season I break the day into blocks and determine what we will be doing at what time, and then we do it. The schedule isn't very flexible; most of the time we won't deviate from it. Throughout the season, at a particular time on a particular day, the team will be doing precisely the same thing for sixteen weeks. Every member of the organization will know exactly what we are doing Wednesday morning at 10:00 A.M., or Thursday at noon, and where they are supposed to be. That isn't going to change. It is as predictable as cold weather in Green Bay in December. Knowledgeable people could tell the time and the day just by looking at what the team is doing at any moment. I operate that way as a means of providing consistency and stability. I want to keep my team off the roller coaster. We don't want peaks and valleys, highs or lows. When sportswriters complained that my teams were regimented, I took it as a compliment. Once we get into our routine a player knows what to expect and when to expect it. The season is a day-to-day, sometimes minute-to-minute grind. But this predictability is an important aspect of preparation. It alleviates a lot of anxiety. No one has to waste time asking questions; instead they can focus specifically on their job.

Even then, though, there are always going to be days when we have to make changes in the schedule. We can't prepare for everything; no one will always know how the football will bounce. But we do try to prepare for the unexpected, too, with what we call a "midstream adjust." Midstream adjust means that if, for whatever reason, our normal schedule is off, we will adapt to the change with poise and focus and without any loss of efficiency. Midstream adjust means that, whatever happens, we accept it, don't get too upset about it, and do whatever is necessary to get back on schedule as quickly as possible. In 2010, while we were in the air flying to Minnesota to play the Vikings, a blizzard hit the Minneapolis area. Our plane was rerouted to Kansas City, and we had to wait there for a decision to be made about when and where we would be playing. The game was finally rescheduled for Sunday night in Minneapolis. We drew up a new schedule to prepare to play Sunday night. But before we could get on our plane, we were told that the Metrodome's roof had collapsed, and instead of playing the Vikings Sunday night in Minneapolis, our game was rescheduled for Monday—in Detroit. We just kept changing and updating the schedule: If we get to the hotel at 5:00 P.M., we'll be meeting at 7:30. If we get there at 6:00 P.M. . . . and on and on. Nobody panicked, nobody got upset, we just kept midstream adjusting. We keep detailed records of our midstream adjust schedule, and if the same issues occur again, we'll be prepared.

Every industry has its busy season and its off-season. Life in the NFL is no different. Our daily schedule during the season is extremely detailed. For me the day usually begins at 5:20 A.M. with a workout, I'll be at my desk at 6:15 and will go until after 10:00 P.M. meetings. Every minute during the week is scheduled. During the season, the deadline for our work is typically (but not always) seven days away. In the off-season, the work is no less intense but the time to achieve our objectives is greater. Our days are not as tightly scheduled.

While during the season we focus each week specifically on accomplishing things we have get done to be properly prepared for our next game, the off-season is the time to take care of long-term projects. There isn't that same time pressure, there isn't a game the next Sunday, but that off-season time has to be used effectively to solve the problems that emerged during the previous season and to prepare for the next one. Each member of the coaching staff has long-term research assignments in the off-season. It starts with self-analysis and research and understanding how to improve. We rewrite the playbook based on our findings to include new concepts studied and learned. We prepare our off-season schedule, as well as our first twelve training camp practices. And, of course, we evaluate and grade personnel for free agency and the college draft.

The schedule is different for players, too, but no less important. There was a time when pro football was a part-time job, and players had other employment in the off-season. That's no longer true; this is a year-round profession. Pro football is not a Monday to Friday, 7:00 A.M. to 4:00 P.M. job.

Great players have a lunch bucket mentality: They work hard and get the job done, whether there are eighty thousand people cheering for them or they're working out by themselves in March. The off-season isn't a vacation; to be ready to do your job, it has to be a conditioning season. If a player doesn't report to training camp in top physical condition and ready to participate, he is already behind the curve. In some cases it's too late for him even before we begin.

The one commitment I do have every off-season is to my wife. Years ago we made a contract that we would spend five days together far away from the office. Those are her five days. Admittedly, I have tried to renegotiate the terms of that agreement, but she has held firm. In fact, she has even lobbied—unsuccessfully, so far—that we expand it to seven days. And during that time, theoretically, I'm not supposed to be working, but somehow I manage to get some work done while fulfilling that contractual obligation.

LONG-TERM PLANNING

Long-term preparation leads directly to success on Sunday afternoon. The actions you take a year or more in advance can have as much impact on the outcome as what you do the day before. Long-term planning puts you in position to win. After being hired by Jacksonville, I had an entire season to build an NFL organization. At that time all we had was a name, a logo, and a trailer. It was an enormous challenge. One of the first things I did was draw up a long-term schedule and insist that we adhere to it strictly. I was afraid that the fact that we had more than a year to build the organization might lull people into believing we had the luxury of time. I tried instead to inject immediacy and intensity into our preparations.

As much as possible during that first year, we prepared as if we already had a team and were playing a complete schedule when, in fact, we were learning to prepare. Among the first things the coaching staff did was hold two complete mock drafts, preparing for both the college draft and the expansion draft. In spring 1995, while the NFL college draft was taking place, we sat and acted as if we were participating in it, going through the entire process. We didn't just think about how we would do it, or make notes. We did a complete draft rehearsal, step-by-step, until we knew exactly what we were doing. At the beginning of the regular season I drew up a schedule, and we game planned against our divisional opponent each week. We made practice schedules for our nonexistent players as if we were getting ready to play a specific opponent. Each weekend throughout the season my assistant coaches and I would go to different college games on Saturday and pro games on Sunday to scout players. On Monday we'd look at tapes of the previous Sunday's NFL games; on

Tuesday we'd lay out our game plan for the weekend. We lived through a complete NFL season, even if we didn't play it. But when it was time to do it for real, our long-term preparation had paid off; we'd already been doing it for a year.

STAY PREPARED FOR AN UNEXPECTED OPPORTUNITY

John Wooden wrote, "The true test of a man's character is what he does when no one is watching." To me, that is the definition of preparation. I've always told my people that playing the game is probably the easiest part of football. The reason we all got into the game in the first place is because we're passionate about playing it. I've had players tell me they would play for free on Sunday afternoons; they are getting paid to practice.

Players pay their dues in the off-season. There are many players who work as hard in the off-season as they do during the year. It isn't easy. There is a lot of temptation to relax, to skip a workout or two. Off-season preparation requires setting long-term goals, making and following a daily workout schedule, even carefully watching their weight. It means making a commitment to success and following through. During the 2011 lockout, Eli Manning continued to work out. But he needed people to throw to. A young receiver who had just barely made our team the previous season named Victor Cruz lived about ten minutes away from Eli. We'd signed him as an undrafted free agent from the University of Massachusetts in 2010. After playing well in the preseason, Victor had injured his hamstring and missed most of the regular season. When we were planning for 2011, in our minds he certainly was not our primary wide receiver. But Victor Cruz took advantage of the time during the lockout, when no one was watching. Whenever Eli called him to come run routes or study the offense, he was right there. While a receiver has a primary route, there are always options that open up. What makes a great quarterback-receiver combination is the quarterback's ability to know exactly what adjustments his receiver will make. "Being on the same page" is the way they refer to it, but it's more than that. It requires being able to read body language on the go, and to make adjustments in the middle of a play, and the only way to learn how to do that is to practice it over and over and over. Victor Cruz wanted to learn, Eli has always been a willing teacher, and the lockout gave them an opportunity to work together. In 2011, Victor Cruz surprised the entire league by becoming one of the top receivers and setting the team record for the most receiving yards in a single season.

As those two players demonstrated, you don't "find" time, you can't "make" time—all you can do is "spend" time. You have to make the most productive use possible of the time that you have. In 2005 the Giants signed linebacker Chase Blackburn as a free agent. He was a reliable player for us for five seasons, and in 2010 he was named our special team's captain. He became a free agent at the end of that season, and we elected not to sign him. When we part ways with a player who has been with us for a while and done a good job, I make a point of telling him how much we appreciate what he did for the team—which we really do. Usually I add, "You know, if you stay in great shape you may get another opportunity. Players are always being sought after, and you never know when someone is going to need a player like you." There are players who take that to heart, and there are other players who basically accept that being released is the end of their careers.

Chase was unable to get a job with another team and had started looking into becoming a substitute math teacher. It was possible his career was over. But he persisted, and he kept working out. Every team brings in unsigned players during the season to work out for the coaching staff, either to address specific needs or to be prepared if a need should arise. Early in 2011 we brought in Chase, just in case we needed a linebacker at some point in the season. It was obvious he had continued training, and we knew that if we did need another linebacker, he would be a viable option. We didn't sign him at that point. But later in the season, after several of our linebackers got hurt, we called Chase, and he joined the team again. When he went into the game the following Sunday, the TV analysts commented that only a few days earlier he'd been "sitting on his couch at home" waiting for the phone to ring. The one thing he hadn't been doing was sitting on his couch. The only thing sitting on the couch prepares you for is sitting on the couch. What he actually had been doing was making the best possible use of his time, preparing for an opportunity to play if a spot opened up on a roster. "I had continued to work hard," he told reporters, "and believe in myself."

When we signed him, we really didn't know how much of a role he would play for us, but in his first week back, against Green Bay, he intercepted an Aaron Rodgers pass. For the remainder of the season he played as well as he had played at any time in his career. He started four of our last five games and all four of our postseason contests. In the fourth quarter of Super Bowl XLVI he made a tremendous defensive play, intercepting a Tom Brady pass on our 8-yard line and preventing a touchdown. That was the only turnover of the entire game. It happened because Chase Blackburn had spent the time preparing when nobody was watching, when he wasn't on any team's payroll, because he intended to be ready if he got an opportunity. If he hadn't done that, it's quite possible the outcome of the Super Bowl might have been different.

There is a motivational saying hanging in just about every

locker room in America: Luck is what happens when opportunity meets preparation. I would put it very differently: *Success* is what happens when opportunity meets preparation. There are Chase Blackburns in the NFL every year, young men who use their time effectively to be prepared for when they do get an opportunity. In 2012, for example, we signed an undrafted free agent defensive end out of Miami named Adewale Ojomo. Our defensive line is one of the strongest aspects of our organization, so most people thought he didn't have much of a chance of making the team. He showed up in camp in great shape, ready to play, and eager to learn. During the preseason, he earned his opportunity and took full advantage of it, getting four sacks. He forced us to pay attention to him. That had nothing to do with luck. This is a perfect example of a young man who succeeded when preparation met opportunity. The more he played, the more confident he became that he could play in the NFL, and he earned a spot on our fifty-three-man roster.

Believe me, I understood exactly what Blackburn had gone through, watching the season go on without him. I understood what Ojomo was playing for. In 2002, after eight seasons at Jacksonville, I was fired. That was devastating for me. Jacksonville had been one of the most successful expansion franchises in NFL history, but we never made it to the Super Bowl. Eventually, ownership thought it needed to make a change. If you invest your whole life in winning and losing, losing practically destroys your self-esteem. Mine was in the tank. I had lost my sense of identity. I was a football coach without a team. I was very fortunate: Several people with whom I'd worked, including Bill Parcells, who was at Dallas at that time, told me they would find a spot for me on their staffs if that was what I wanted to do. But I was geared to work as a head coach, not to look for work. This was the first time in a decade that I had unscheduled time. There was no place I had to be. In essence, this was a test of my program. How well I used my time would determine my future.

I drew up a schedule for myself and I kept to it. In March, I went to the predraft scouting combine in Indianapolis, which is as close to an NFL convention as there is. While I was there I ran into Ernie Accorsi, the Giants' general manager at the time, who said to me, "What are you doing here? You don't coach a team." To which I replied, "I will." During the preseason I visited five different training camps and sat in on team meetings. It was important for me to stay involved, to be prepared to take advantage of an opportunity. Being ready was my job, and I treated it as such.

When the season started I would spend all day Saturday watching college football. On Sunday morning I would go to Mass, and when I got home I would bid the family good-bye, go to the family room to watch the early games, and come downstairs after the Sunday night game had ended. I'd usually watch the games, by myself and take notes, evaluating players, looking at coaches' strategies, wondering which jobs were going to be available. I can't begin to estimate how many notebooks I filled that season. Every Monday morning I would call Mike Perkins, the Jaguars' video director, and tell him what games I wanted to look at. Can you get me a tape of San Francisco's passing game? I'd like to look at Green Bay's running game. Mike and his assistants would make those tapes for me, and Tuesday morning I'd meet him in the parking lot of a Target and he would hand me a box of tapes. I'd spend the rest of the week analyzing those games.

For the first time in my career I worked at home. That was difficult, as there were a lot of distractions, and I had to remain focused. I had always made a point of reminding my coaches that there are many things that can get in the way of what we were trying to accomplish and they can't become distracted and allow those things to take their minds off the goal. Distractions can sap your energy, effort, and desire, and when those things are affected, your efficiency is down. Now it was my turn to take my own advice. And as hard as it was for me to be at home that season, focusing on finding a new head coaching job, it was maybe harder on Judy. As she said later, "One thing we found out that year was that I was not anxious for him to retire."

With two games left in the regular season, the Giants'

head coach, Jim Fassel, announced his own firing. Several days later the Giants' executive vice president, John Mara, called and asked if I was interested in interviewing for the New York Giants job. Of course I was. There were several serious candidates. I was interviewed by John Mara and Ernie Accorsi. Ernie remembered our meeting at the combine, and I suspect that was a factor in the Giants' decision to hire me. He knew that I was prepared to go to work immediately. I didn't have to "waste" time catching up with the league. I hadn't simply passed the time while I was unemployed; I had used it productively to prepare for whatever happened in the future.

There are few things that bother me more than wasting time. When it makes sense, in fact, I'll try to expand the use of my time by doing more than one thing. For example, when I'm driving, rather than listening to the radio I'll put on motivational tapes and stories to try to find material I can present to the team. Some kids grow up listening to music when they ride in the car with their parents; mine grew up listening to things like the greatest speeches of General George Patton.

People are not surprised to hear that I don't respond well to wasting time—even when it's my own fault. I played college football for Ben Schwartzwalder at Syracuse University. I was a running back and played in the same backfield as Hall of Fame members Floyd Little and Larry Csonka. I was in the lineup because they needed eleven guys. In 1974 Frank Maloney replaced Coach Schwartzwalder at Syracuse. By that time I'd been at RIT for five years and had established a young, aspiring football program. I knew Frank Maloney intended to hire his own staff, so I approached him at an alumni function and introduced myself, then said, "If you're looking for assistants, you know I'd love to talk to you about it."

The prospect of returning to Syracuse as a member of the coaching staff was very exciting for me. In early March, Coach Maloney called and asked me to come up to the university for an interview. Our plan was to discuss an open defensive position on his staff. My dream was coming true. I had a chance to become an assistant coach at my alma mater. This was the opportunity I had spent every day of the last five years at RIT preparing for. As I always do, I made very specific plans for that night. It would take me about two hours to drive to Syracuse. I made my schedule, writing down everything I had to do. I had it timed perfectly: I was going to race home from RIT, shower, shave, put on my coat and tie, jump in my car, drive the two hours, and arrive at Manley field house precisely at 6:00 P.M. to meet Coach Maloney. It was all planned, like clockwork. Better than clockwork, Coughlin Time.

I followed my schedule perfectly. Drove home. Took a shower. Got dressed. Kissed Judy and our two young children, Keli and Timmy, for good luck and was ready to go—but I couldn't find my car keys. We had only one car—and no keys. When I got home I'd put them down in the usual spot, and they were gone. Gone. It was obvious that one of our kids had picked them up to play with and dropped them somewhere. Judy and I began searching. The clock kept moving. Time was beyond my control. The most important night of my professional life, and my schedule was falling apart. I started sweating. Big sweat stains soaked through my shirt into my jacket. As we turned the house upside down looking for those keys, I kept glancing at the clock, trying to will it to stop moving. I couldn't believe this was happening to me, the person who had always been so meticulous about not wasting a second. It was like a terrible joke. Eventually it became obvious I wasn't going to make it to Syracuse on time for the interview.

I had no choice: I called Coach Maloney and explained the situation to him. For a person who lives his life in control, admitting I had no control was difficult for me. To my relief, when I finished telling him the story he started laughing, telling me, "I've got my own kids." To me it was a colossal failure; for him it was a real-life story.

Judy eventually found the keys in her bobby pin container under the bathroom sink, where our son Timothy had dropped them. Two weeks later I got to Syracuse, on time, and was hired to be the quarterback coach. But four decades later I still can close my eyes and feel that anxiety in the pit of my stomach. I'm still trying to honor the commitment I made to myself to never waste my time or, for that matter, anybody else's, but whenever I start taking myself very seriously, I remember that somehow I survived the night when my schedule collapsed. Always take your job seriously, but not yourself!

THREE

Success Is in the Details

It's the little details that are vital. Little things make big things happen.

—John Wooden

Knowledge is the heartbeat of preparation. The amount of information you can provide to your people will be directly proportional to your success. At the beginning of every season our coaches are reminded that each of them must become a person of detail. As we tell them, "Be thorough—establish a logical file system, then record and file all football- and player-related information." It is always possible that other teams will hit harder than we do, although we try to make sure that doesn't happen. It is also possible that they might put more talent on the field than we do, and that has happened. But the one thing we always know for certain is that no one will be better prepared than we are. No one is going to know more about us than we know about them.

The biggest pieces can be broken down into the smallest parts. It was Benjamin Franklin who pointed out that "little strokes fell great oaks." If you intend to win, no matter what it is you're doing, you have to pay attention to those details.

LEARN THE DETAILS

The margin between success and failure in the NFL, in most enterprises in fact, is so small that a little bit of information can make all the difference. A quarter-second hesitation, a half step in the wrong direction, can determine the success of a play, which can make the difference in the outcome of the game, and that one game can affect the entire season. In this area, professional football is no different from any other competitive industry. Success requires gathering as much information as possible from all possible sources, using it to determine both your own and your opponent's strengths and weaknesses, and then figuring out how to pit your strengths against his weaknesses. Why is your competitor scoring more points or selling more products than you are? What does he do that you should be doing? In business, this is known as market research. In football, it's scouting your opponent.

Basically, we know our own strengths. We spend a considerable amount of time during the season analyzing our own team. So we know what our opponent is seeing. We know what we do well and where we have to do better. What we're looking for each week is the information that will tell us where our opponent is most vulnerable. Where do we want to attack him? What does he do very well? What does he do poorly? Where do we have an edge? Only after you have all of that information can you really begin laying out a strategy, planning how to use what you do best to exploit their weaknesses. After four seasons playing for the Jaguars, tight end Pete Mitchell signed with the Giants in 1999. "I didn't regret leaving," he later said, "but I missed Tom's details. Before every Jacksonville game our coaches would give us these finite readouts on the other team—what their linebackers did on third down with less than 3 yards, on third down with more than 3 yards and less than 6 yards, or third down and more than 9 yards. So on third down we knew exactly what to expect. I got to other teams and they didn't give us that information. I would get in a game and find myself thinking, 'I wish I knew a little more about this third down situation.' I came to realize that Tom wasn't driving us crazy with these details for no reason."

In the information-gathering process, every detail matters. No matter how much you learn, there will always be something more. As much time as the coaching staff spends working with the players on the practice field, we spend considerably more time accumulating knowledge from every possible source about our opponent. We study videotape, we read and reread scouting reports, we pour over statistics. We scout their games and speak to other coaches who have played them. Then we put it all together to create our strategy, our game plan. There's a common football expression, "The hay's in the barn," which means you've done all you can do, and the work is done. In our facility, the hay never gets into the barn. It's those late nights when you're sitting alone in your office, looking at rows of numbers or watching the same footage over and over and trying to make sense of it, that you earn the right to win. The reality is that no matter how much you've done, there is always something else you can do. There is always more to be learned. Always. And you never know what little piece of information will make the difference between winning and losing. While we were preparing for Super Bowl XLII, we noticed that when the Patriots offense lined up, their center looked at each of our linebackers to see where they were positioned, then looked away. He never checked back to see if they had moved. We told our middle linebacker, Kawika Mitchell, that when that center looked at him he should start dropping back as if he were going into coverage, but as soon as the center turned away, he should attack. "You should be wide open," Spagnuolo told him. "We're going to get a sack out of it."

Early in the second quarter Mitchell did exactly as he had been told and we had practiced—and got the first of our five sacks that day on Tom Brady.

Meticulous planning makes a difference. There are people who believe I can be obsessive, but I have a passion for my work. That's a gift. The complexities of the game of football have fascinated and intrigued me my whole life. I've spent more than four decades in pursuit of perfection, even while knowing the whole time that it doesn't exist. I started doing this at RIT, when my entire staff consisted of me and a couple of volunteers who showed up after work in the afternoon. I was responsible for everything, from pounding in the stakes that hold the ropes that went around the field to coaching the game. I was in charge of every detail. I was the one who got on the phone to other coaches and made up our future schedule. At that time we only had rudimentary scouting reports, most of which were handwritten and copied on the mimeograph machine. We were working with a very small budget, but we provided our players with as much information about our opponents as possible. We watched all the film we could get. We made extensive notes and handed them out. That preparation and attention to detail eventually paid off. We played Hobart during our second year, one of the top five Division III teams in the nation. They had two All-American running backs, and on the line outweighed us by about thirty pounds per man. "Nobody had ever heard of us," one of my linebackers, Ken Wegner, later recalled. "That game it finally sunk in that we knew what we were doing. On defense, we knew the plays they were going to run before they snapped the ball. By looking at where their tight end was standing I knew whether they were going to run inside or attempt a pass. Our level of preparation allowed us to overcome their size, experience, and talent." The game ended in a 14–14 tie, which was a big upset. We actually could have won that game, but Hobart blocked a punt that led to a touchdown.

In my world there is no such thing as too much information. Eli Manning summed it up when he said, "Preparation is addictive. There is no better feeling in the world than coming up to the line of scrimmage on third down, looking at the way the defense is set up, and knowing not only exactly what they are going to do, but that you have the perfect play to counter that. Once you've experienced that feeling of calling signals totally confident that you are running the perfect play, you want to get back there again and again. You see how all the hard work you've done on the practice field, all the hours you've spent studying, and all the preparation you've done come together at that one moment and makes the game look simple. The more work you do, the more the game slows down."

We've always tried to give our players all the information that might be useful. "We would joke about how much information we had," Tony Boselli remembers. "Before the game started we knew everything from the weather forecast to the names of the officials and what penalties they called most often. We were prepared. There was no stone left unturned. As an offensive lineman, I knew what our opponent's defense liked to do on every down and what they did from every position on the field. In the bigger picture, I knew their turnover ratio and their success in preventing first downs from every part of the field. Then we broke it down further, to the individual tendencies of the player I was lining up against. We rarely were surprised."

The Saturday night before a Sunday game, when we meet with the team, we give them what we call "the keys to victory." These are the things we have to do to win. This isn't unusual; pretty much every coach does the same thing. The difference is that their list usually includes four or five main points while ours might include fifteen or twenty keys: This team hasn't won a game when they've turned the ball over twice or more; we have to score in the red zone; punt the ball long and out of bounds, so there's zero return yardage. Obviously not every detail applies to every player, but we want the whole team to be prepared. We know we are giving our players a lot more information than many of them can absorb, and that is fine. We also know they will pick out and remember the five or six that can be especially useful to them during the game. Some of those keys might apply to special teams players, others may be important only to the offensive line, still others might be useful to defensive backs. Of all the keys that we provide, only about five of them will apply to the whole team.

No matter what job you're doing, or what plans you're making, it can be broken down into numerous small details. And any one of those details can make a significant difference. When I was a position coach I broke down the requirements of that position into numerous smaller skills, then worked on each one of them separately. In 1976, I was Frank Maloney's quarterbacks coach at Syracuse. Just as I would years later with Doug Flutie, I was working with our starter, Bill Hurley, and his backup, Randy Edsall, on their footwork. The faster a quarterback can drop back and get set in the pocket, the more time he has to look at the field in front of him. I told Randy over and over that when a quarterback is under center, both of his feet should be pointing at high noon on the face of an imaginary clock, and that when a right-handed quarterback takes his first step, his right foot should be at four o'clock. Doing it that way enables the quarterback to get set up as quickly and firmly as possible. Randy was having trouble with it; his first step back was at three thirty, not four o'clock. When I focused on that little difference over and over, he looked at me like I had come from another planet. It was a very small detail, but it made a difference in how quickly he could drop back and get set. He practiced it again and again, and eventually that forced repetition of detail made it natural.

No matter what you're trying to accomplish, details can make the difference. If you're selling ice cream, you should know what happens to your product at varying temperatures. If you're driving a truck, you'd better know which gas stations are open at 2:00 A.M. If you're coaching a football team, you'd better know the range of your opponent's place-kicker on a windy day. When we were planning the new facility in Jacksonville, I got involved in every detail, from the number of toilets in the coaches' locker room to the type of chairs we would buy for the meeting rooms and how we would set them up. I wanted to know how far the people sitting in the front row were going to be from the video screen in the team room. When I asked Mike Perkins that question, he looked at me like I was crazy. "How far away does Kansas City sit?" I asked him. "How far away does New England sit?" I wanted to know how the better run organizations operated. How many feet from the screen was most comfortable for the players? What distance did their coaches prefer? How far away was too far? Mike probably spent two days calling people in those different organizations, asking them to measure the distance between the front row and the screen. We settled on seven feet.

Everything counts. Before the Giants played our first game in the new MetLife Stadium in 2010 we conducted studies to determine field conditions. We made charts to see how the shadows moved across the field in the afternoon so we would know when each portion of the field was going to be in sun or in shadow. We set wind gauges in all four corners and the middle of the field, so we would have some idea of what kind of wind conditions we could expect in the stadium and when to expect them. We wanted to be prepared for as many weather conditions as possible so we would know which end of the field to pick when kicking off in early

December and what wind conditions our placekicker should expect at 4:30 in the afternoon. When you've got a fourth down and short yardage on your opponent's 35-yard line, and you're trying to decide whether to go for a first down or a field goal or punt the ball away, this information can be very important.

The same thing is true when we're playing on the road. I always give my players as much information as possible about the environment we're walking into, everything from the facilities in the locker room to the quality of the field surface. It all matters. We always tell our players the type of footing they should expect to find, whether it's natural grass or FieldTurf or some other type of artificial surface. If players are prepared for that they don't have to worry about it during the game, allowing them to focus on executing their assignments.

We are always looking for that edge. Knowing the details can sometimes let you challenge the conventional wisdom. At one point I read that the Baltimore Ravens were apparently doing research into sleep patterns so they could be better prepared when they played on the road in a different time zone, especially when they traveled to the West Coast and had a three-hour time difference. A time-zone change has always been perceived to be an advantage to the home team. Most often, when an East Coast team is playing a Sunday game on the West Coast, they fly out there on Friday to give themselves a day to get accustomed to the time difference.

But after we'd lost a game on the West Coast on the very last play, and I thought it was because we had been worn down, I decided to do it differently. Scientifically this doesn't hold water, but it has worked for us: We fly out the day before the game. When we arrive, we have our meetings, and by eight o'clock on the West Coast, eleven o'clock our time, our players are in a prone position. They have an opportunity to get extra sleep if they allow themselves to do that. Maybe it's a small thing, but my experience has been that it does make a difference.

We'll review every aspect of the game in search of that elusive advantage. We even analyze the tendencies of the officials. During the week I'll get a report from our senior director of football operations, Jon Berger, telling me about the people scheduled to work our game. Just like players, NFL officials have specific tendencies. Some of them look for interior lineman holding, and others might regularly see blocks in the back on punt returns. We tell our players how the officials are ranked, what penalties they tend to call and how often they call them, and even how often their calls are overturned on a challenge. If I'm thinking about throwing a challenge flag but I'm not certain whether or not to do it, it helps to know that this team of officials has overturned about 60 percent of challenged calls.

There are several reasons we focus on details. First, obviously, we want the team to have that information. We want them to be confident that there is a reason behind every decision we make, we're not just standing out there making guesses, and those decisions are based on good information. And second, I want the coaching staff to do the data mining without having to be told what to do. They have to be ready to respond to any question at any time with an accurate and detailed answer. The difference between sitting seven feet or eight feet away from the screen may not be significant, but knowing I may ask for details like that will keep the staff focusing on them. I don't want either the players or the coaching staff to ever become complacent.

STUDY THE NUMBERS

The details can always be found in the numbers. The value of statistics in sports was illustrated by the book and movie *Moneyball*, which showed how baseball's Oakland A's used statistics rather than traditional methods to build a very competitive team. Statistics are a big part of what we do. We spend a considerable amount of time breaking down both our own team and our opponents statistically to try to pinpoint our advantages. Statistics are the language of football; numbers can describe teams and players in tremendous detail. Any company in any industry will benefit from compiling a detailed statistical analysis of their competition as well as that of their own company. Understanding what those numbers mean, how they can be pushed up, or what it means when they drop down can be the difference between success and failure. There is a tremendous amount of detail in those numbers, and you just have to be smart enough to speak the language.

Just about every aspect of the game can be expressed as a number, and that number can be used as a basis of comparison. The statistics we use can be as broad as a team's win-loss record or as precise as the percent of third down completions a quarterback will throw to his tight end, wide receivers, or running backs. Statistics can tell us both tendencies, such as the percentage breakdown of the number of times our opponent will call either a pass or a run on third down in the red zone, or specifics, like the number of passing touchdowns they've given up in their previous four games. Statistics allow you to make reasonable projections about your opponent's game plan, about what they will do in various scenarios, and based on this we try to figure out how to counterattack. The numbers will tell you what you have to do to prevent that other team from doing what they do best.

The key is to understand the language of percentages, and to be able to find in it the most important tendencies. The more hours I spend looking at the numbers, slicing them, dicing them, cutting them up, and putting them together, the more detailed of a story they tell me. The better we understand that story, the easier it is to put the odds in our favor. If, for example, our opponent has targeted a specific receiver on second and long in the red zone, we have a pretty good idea of what we need to defend when we're in that situation. Every team has access to the same numbers, so the real art is in how you use them. For starters, the numbers give us a pretty good idea of how to prepare. Statistically we found that short yardage situations occur only two or three plays a game, so we were spending too much time preparing for situations that rarely took place on the field. We were wasting time. Therefore, we were better able to plot our practice time accordingly.

The numbers have to be interpreted. Numbers without context can be very misleading. For example, we might see that an opponent is ranked twenty-eighth in rushing. That's good for us; for some reason they don't have an effective rushing game. But then we have to understand why. It might be because their featured running back has been out with an injury, but this player is coming back for our game. There is a reason for every statistic; understanding the why of it is essential.

We also spend a lot of time looking at our own numbers. Self-scouting enables us to identify our own strengths and weaknesses, as well as our tendencies. If we see we're doing something exceptionally well, we're probably going to keep doing it until somebody figures out how to stop us. When you're selling a lot of cereal, just keep putting those boxes on the shelves until they end up sitting there. It's logical:

Determine what you do best and keep doing it until it isn't working anymore. But usually, when we see that we've become predictable, we try to shake things up. We can even use that knowledge to our advantage. When the numbers point out where we're not doing well, in practice we'll focus on solving those problems. We may even be able to use it to our advantage. We'll show our opponent the formation they're expecting to see in a certain situation, but then we'll run something totally unexpected from it.

We always feed our players a steady diet of numbers. We want them to understand why we do certain things at certain times. We give them something to hang their hats on, something that might give them a little extra confidence that they are going into the game well prepared. A player who believes he is prepared is a confident player, and a confident player will play better. While we were preparing for Super Bowl XLII, we spent hours and hours going through all of Patriots' quarterback Tom Brady's stats. No matter how we looked at them, they were impressive. He is a great player, and his numbers reflected that. That wasn't a big secret, but what we wanted to do was give our players confidence in our game plan. So we highlighted specific aspects of his game. We broke down his game by the numbers: Is he more successful passing to his right or to his left? What does he like to do on third down and 4-to-6 yards, third and 7-through-10 yards, and third and 11-plus yards? Who is his favorite receiver in short yardage situations? How often is he able to draw line-men offsides with a hard count? These were the types of de-tails our players had before the game started. It's the type of information they have every week. Knowledge builds confi-dence, and confidence is a huge asset in any situation.

We weren't going to be able to prevent Tom Brady from completing a high percentage of his passes. We knew that. But we wanted to cut down the extra yards his receivers gained after they caught the ball. Yards gained after a recep-tion is a key stat in the NFL. Brady is a great quarterback, but great receivers like Randy Moss and Wes Welker made him even more dangerous. One stat that stood out to us was that Brady hadn't been hit very much during the whole season. Their offensive line was so good, and he had such a quick re-lease, that other teams had rarely gotten to him. There was a reason the Patriots were 18–0 in 2007 and a heavy favorite to complete a perfect season. But looking at the stats, we decided our game plan was to make him uncomfortable in the pocket.

Our game plan was built from a thousand details. We watched hours of tape, went over the scouting reports, and pored over the numbers. Our defensive game plan had three primary objectives. First, we wanted to hit Tom Brady as much as possible, so we decided to blitz at every opportunity. Even if we couldn't get to Brady, we wanted to keep pressure on him, disrupt his rhythm, and force him to get rid of the ball more quickly than he wanted to. Doing that would help us achieve our second objective, which was to prevent him from completing a pass longer than 20 yards. And third, we wanted their receivers tackled at the spot they caught the ball. No add-on yardage. When Welker caught a 5-yard slant, we couldn't let him gain an additional 10 yards. For the two weeks before the game, that's what we emphasized: Hit Brady at every opportunity, make him throw short passes, and stop his receivers with no additional yardage.

In the game we hit Brady eighteen times; we hit him nine times in his first eighteen attempts. We sacked him five times, and he didn't complete a pass longer than 19 yards. And because the players performed on the field, we held New England to a season low of fourteen points. All the little things we had done, the mountain of numbers we had compiled, examined, and distilled into our game plan, resulted in the most important numbers of all—in a game considered one of the greatest upsets in Super Bowl history, we beat the undefeated Patriots, 17–14.

STUDY YOUR COMPETITION

Anybody in any business who intends to be successful better learn as much about his competitors as he knows about his own company. In addition to statistics, we get a tremendous amount of information from scouting reports and video. Beginning early Monday morning during the season and continuing pretty much throughout the week we'll watch a tremendous amount of film of our upcoming opponent. We have a video department that prepares the clip packages we request, from one player in action against several different opponents, so we can see how other teams have played him, to every third down and long yardage play for the entire season. I don't stop reviewing; on Sunday when I get to the stadium, I look at video on my laptop. Today's technology allows us to develop as many "cut ups" as we can imagine and use. The trick is to emphasize the most pertinent information concerning the opponent. I'll study cut ups a dozen times or until I understand exactly what the opponent is doing. And it isn't just me; most of our coaching staff is doing the same thing.

Every week the coaching staff meets with the players to go over what we've learned from our film study. We'll show our receivers a compilation of every single pass thrown at a certain corner the entire season, knowing that after looking at him making thirty or forty plays, they'll get a pretty good feel for what he likes to do. "Look at this guy," I'll tell our receivers, "he's very aggressive. If you do a good job selling your route you can get him to try to jump it." Or I might warn them, "This guy is strong. After you've made a catch, he'll try to wrestle you for the ball."

Our players also will spend a lot of time during the week looking at footage, mostly tape of the player they are going to line up against. We provide video for every position, including the special teams. We take footage from two angles—from the end zone and from the sideline at the 50-yard line—so they will be able to identify their opponent. There is no question that if you watch enough footage of a player you can learn something about him that can give you an edge. It might be the way he sets his feet when he's going to move in a certain direction or the fact that a quarterback opens his hands an instant before the snap. Even in a game that rewards teamwork and unity, every player is unique. Every player does something just a little bit different.

The fact is that the more you know about your competition in general, and the individuals working there, the more success you'll have in reaching your objective. That's just as true for an entrepreneur as it is for an interior linemen. So you have to gather every possible scrap of information about that competition and use it to create your winning strategy. But even in a world where amazing technology is readily available, where you can look at cold numbers and get expert analysis, the one thing that should never be overlooked is the human element.

In football, our scouts provide that human element. They provide insights and updates that won't show up on film or in the stats. Each scout is assigned to a team, and during the season they are responsible for being as up-to-date as the weather on those teams. A scout is like a marketing expert for a certain line of products. His job is to know as much as possible about them. If one part changes, he needs to know it. A scout is the person who actually goes into the store, watches shoppers take items off the shelf, and tries to understand why a woman picks one brand instead of another. So while film shows execution, scouts report on the human element. They'll go through the opposition lineup player by player; who's injured, who's playing at less than full capacity, who has been playing especially well or who can be beat in certain situations. Scouts also will talk about gadget or gimmick plays an opponent uses, who's throwing the ball—the wide receiver? The halfback? Can the punter run or will he throw the ball? Before the Giants played Dallas in December 2011, a game we had to win to stay in contention for a play-off spot, the scouting report pointed out that it was possible the Cowboys' rookie placekicker could be iced. A week earlier against Arizona he had made what should have been a game-winning 49-yard field goal with six seconds left in the game. But his own coach had called a time-out just before the kick. The placekicker then missed his second attempt, and the Cardinals won the game in overtime.

We decided that if our game came down to a field goal attempt at the end, we would freeze the kicker. We would call a time-out before he kicked to increase the mental pressure on him. Statistically, freezing a placekicker didn't appear to make much of a difference, but we knew his failure at the end of the Arizona game was now in his head. If we had a chance to remind him of that, perhaps put just a little bit of doubt there, who knows what could happen?

With seconds left in the game, we were leading 37–34. The Cowboys lined up to attempt a 47-yard field goal that would tie the score. An instant before the kicker successfully drilled it between the uprights for what would have been a game-tying field goal, I called a time-out. His kick didn't count. As I knew from our preparation, this was exactly the same situation he had been in a week earlier; he missed that kick, which cost the Cowboys the game. That miss certainly put additional pressure on this kick. When the ball was snapped for his second attempt, maybe there was an instant of hesitation. Whatever happened, Jason Pierre-Paul managed to get a hand on the ball. The kick wobbled off to the side. No good. We ran off the field with the win that kept our play-off hopes alive.

We do rely on scouting reports, but it's also important to remember that football is a game played by humans and evaluated by humans, and humans make errors. Victor Cruz didn't even get drafted, for example. We signed him only because we needed to have a certain number of receivers in training camp, and one scout told us he was a player worth looking at. That has served as a great reminder to me that in addition to compiling all the numbers and doing a variety of analyses, winning might eventually come down to one person saying, "Give that guy a chance. He's got heart."

MAKE A BIG DEAL ABOUT THE SMALL THINGS

We have always tried to bring that same level of attention to detail to every aspect of our organization. Creating a first-class organization requires doing everything at a first-class level. We insist on excellence. If you allow people to get lazy or sloppy about the small things, eventually they will begin taking the big things for granted, and that attitude will pervade the entire system. Focusing on the small things allows you to prevent them from becoming big problems. I insist that our players wear ties when traveling, for example, to remind them that we are on a serious business trip. We represent the New York Giants and we must give significance to game day. Our appearance is representative of our pride and professionalism.

When we were building the organization in Jacksonville, the initial impression anyone was going to get about our level of professionalism was going to be the way we operated our first training camp. If it was chaotic, if people didn't seem to know what they were doing, if we lacked equipment, the obvious impression would be that we weren't prepared. Jeff Lageman was a six-year NFL veteran when he signed with us as a free agent, and when he showed up at that first camp, he didn't know what to expect. As he recalls two decades later, "I think everyone was wondering what we were getting into. There's no question we were all very curious, and probably a little anxious. My first morning in camp I went down to the training table for breakfast. The quality of the food is always a good way to judge an organization. When I ran into Tom, he asked me what I thought about it. I told him it was outstanding; in fact, it was so good that if I wasn't careful I'd end up gaining ten pounds. But then I added that the coffee wasn't very good, because it wasn't.

"The next morning, the very next morning, the entire coffee system had been changed and the coffee was top-notch. What was impressive was that they would take care of such a little thing so quickly. But it definitely made the point. Any doubt I might have had about the way the organization was going to be run ended right there. It was obvious they were well prepared and intended to run a first-class operation."

Obviously, little things like the quality of the coffee can be used to convey or reinforce a message. We were making it clear by focusing on small details that the Jacksonville

Jaguars were going to run a first-class operation. I've always emphasized how important it is to create a professional environment, a place where players and coaches want to come, a place where the only thing they have to worry about is doing their job. I have this rule: When players return for the start of the season, something will have been changed, replaced, or upgraded. We might have installed new carpeting, or repainted a faded or chipped wall a brighter color, or put new computers in the players' lounge. We're making the point that we are aware of everything going on, and that they are members of a first-class organization.

In the end, of course, the only thing that most people see is the big picture. When we look at a van Gogh painting, we appreciate its beauty, but very few people think about the thousands of individual brushstrokes that it took to create that one great image. All of those countless tiny details come together to create a magnificent work of art. In anything you do, your ability to focus on the details and bring them all together will determine your success or failure.

FOUR

Communication

Say what you mean, and mean what you say.

—GENERAL GEORGE PATTON

Success begins with communication. In any environment, effectively communicating your message to your organization, clearly and concisely, is absolutely essential. It isn't just what you are communicating, it's also how well you communicate. The right message delivered the wrong way has no value. If people don't get your message, you're wasting both your time and their time. Earning the right to win requires establishing solid relationships with your fellow workers. You all need to be on the same page.

SEND A CLEAR AND POSITIVE MESSAGE

In December 2011, the Giants played the Washington Redskins at MetLife Stadium. It was a game we needed to win to secure a play-off spot. Our record was 7–6, we'd lost four of our previous five games, and some reporters were writing that if we didn't make the play-offs I would be fired. The Redskins were 4–9 and were playing for their pride. It was one of those "must-win" games for us—although to me every game is a must-win game—and we played very poorly. They beat us 23–10. Everything that could have gone wrong went wrong. We played without passion. To say I was disappointed doesn't begin to accurately describe my feelings. It's always been hard for me to know what to say to my team in the locker room five minutes after a loss. That's a really tough time. Everyone's emotions are raw. People are angry and upset. This was a very bad loss for us, and I knew what the players expected to hear from me. Nobody expected me to be polite.

I have a temper. I tend to say what I think. I can't help it; that's just the way I am. Earlier in my career, if I had to face this situation, there is no question of how I would have responded. I would have exploded. I would have focused on all the negative things that happened during the game. And maybe I would have lost the team for the rest of the season. But this time I didn't. I made my feelings clear—we were a better team than we were showing—but I focused on the fact that we still had control of our destiny. I reminded them that if we won the next two games we would be division champions. I told our players, "Get your heads up. Get the frowns off your faces."

Instead of dwelling on the loss, I wanted them to start looking forward to our next game. We turned the page and got right to work preparing for the must-win game the following Sunday.

Giants' cornerback Cory Webster explained that best when he told reporters, "Everybody's got a steely eyed focus. We don't have a long-term memory. We use the short-term memory. We call it FIDO—forget it and drive on."

I wasn't always able to be a coach who swallowed his anger and looked ahead. During my career, I've had to change the way I communicate with my players. Early on my method was pretty simple: The coach speaks, the players listen. My way or the highway. The coach tells his players what to do and they do it. It was very much the same way in football as it was in any business: The boss is always right. I had learned the art of communication from my parents, and from the nuns in elementary school, who basically communicated with a pointer to your knuckles. Starting in Jacksonville I earned a reputation for being tough, taciturn, and demanding. Tom Tyrant, the writers called me, or Technical Tom. When I was criticized for my methods, I told reporters, "This isn't Club Med." I think the people who played for me those years would say that while they respected me, they probably didn't like me very much. Frankly, I didn't care about that, as long as they listened to me. They did, and it worked. That's the way most coaches communicated at that time. Old school.

Nobody ever described Vince Lombardi as a warm and friendly guy on the football field. But times changed, the world changed, and I didn't. "Listen to me or else" was no longer considered the most effective means of getting through to your team.

When the Giants hired me in 2004 the players knew all about my reputation. From the very beginning, Michael Strahan stood up against me, probably representing the whole team, and fought me every step. He thought I was a tyrant, that I didn't care at all about the players. He thought my attitude was too rigid and my rules didn't make sense, complaining, "What difference does it make what color socks you wear to practice?" Whatever I did, he questioned.

It was a bad situation. I wanted to change it, but I didn't know how. It's not easy to change; you can't wake up one day and become another person. You can't "act" differently. Try that, and everyone will see right through you. Change has to be real; it has to come from your core. At the end of the 2004 season, Kurt Warner became a free agent. He had opened the year as our starting quarterback, but I'd replaced him mid-season with rookie Eli Manning. Kurt Warner had been great about it; he is a man of great character, and he had accepted the situation professionally, continuing to contribute to the team by working with Eli. After the season he asked if we could sit down and talk. During that meeting I asked him to make a list of all the things he thought I needed to do better as a coach. I'd never done anything like that before, but I was trying to see the problems from a player's point of view. "Don't hold back," I told him.

I expected him to write down three or four suggestions. Instead he wrote page after page of what I needed to do to improve my relationship with the players. He didn't hold back, telling me that he knew I wouldn't hold it against him, because he did it with my best interests at heart. A key point of that list was: Rather than just making rules and enforcing them, I should explain to the players why that rule is important to me. Not defend it, explain it. As he said, "Some players will still think the rules are silly, but they'll figure, 'He wants us five minutes early because it's important to him. No big deal.'" Basically, he suggested that I swallow my pride and find a way to really connect to the players—every player, from the biggest star to the players on the practice squad.

I kept that list, and on occasion I still refer to it. If I really wanted to communicate with our players, Kurt emphasized, I had to stop being so negative. Being critical is part of a coach's job. A coach spends at least part of every day correcting players, helping them improve their game. When a player continues to make the same mental errors or repeats the same physical mistakes over and over, a coach has to deal with it. Which I did, often very loudly and in what would be referred to as "colorful" language. I learned how to do that from some real masters of the art, and some of those times I had learned because I was on the receiving end of a tirade. So I knew what it feels like to be criticized. It isn't pleasant. What I didn't know was how to do it differently.

Being negative is an easy habit for any leader to fall into, and I had to learn that it wasn't necessarily the most effective way to communicate. It took me some time to figure out that too often it just didn't work. It doesn't create a positive relationship, it doesn't motivate a player to play harder for you or work harder for you. Mostly, being negative causes resentment and makes it even harder to communicate. In my profession, like in most businesses, if you've got good people working for you, those people are driven to succeed. Their character, pride, and ambition motivate them far better than any of my words could. And when a person is driven, he or she is the hardest person in the world on themselves. They don't need me standing behind them yelling in their ear to know that they made a mistake. When you have hardworking, disciplined people like Eli Manning working for you, why would you ever yell at him, no matter how he has played? He's ten times harder on himself than I'm ever going to be. All negativity does is create more negativity—without being particularly effective. I had to learn that I could accomplish a lot more by being reasonable, or even positive. I have to admit, I don't remember that all the time, but I definitely have gotten better. When the result isn't what I want, rather than coming down hard, I try to focus on the effort. John

Wooden believed that a coach should evaluate effort. If the effort is good, then a coach's job is to try to find a way to help them improve the result.

GETTING UPSET DOESN'T SOLVE THE PROBLEM

Probably the most difficult thing for me to change has been learning how to better express my frustration and my disappointment. It's hard for me, with my Irish ancestry, not to be emotional and vocalize my feelings. But most of the time getting angry and yelling communicates only one thing: you're angry. Generally, though, it doesn't help achieve your goals. Once you start screaming, shouting, and turning red in the face, no one is going to be paying much attention to what you're trying to tell them. Instead they're thinking, "Get this guy away from me." People on the receiving end of an angry rant often don't focus on the specifics of what went wrong. They already know what went wrong. What they need is guidance about correcting it to make certain it doesn't happen again.

I try to remember that, although sometimes it isn't easy for me. I do express my anger. At times it got out of control. I didn't just get angry, I erupted. On the sidelines, when an official made what I believed was a bad call, I let him know it, loudly. When a player made a mistake, I wasn't shy about telling him what I thought about it. As a member of my staff pointed out, it was ironic; I would drill it into my team over and over and over that they had to maintain control on the field no matter what happened, that they had to keep their poise, and that I did not want any penalties—while at the same time I was screaming, yelling, throwing clipboards, and losing control and my poise.

One Sunday afternoon early in my career as a head coach, my wife was watching our game on television at home with my mother. After what I considered to be a bad call, the camera focused on me just as I let loose a long string of expletives. You didn't have to be an expert lip reader to know what I was saying. Judy was appalled. How was my mother going to react to seeing her son cursing on national TV? "Oh, don't worry about it," my mother said. "I've heard that word many times before."

While many people won't believe it, I actually have a good relationship with many NFL officials. At least some of the NFL officials. This is definitely a different type of communication. Usually, when I'm speaking to, or sometimes yelling at, officials, I'm trying to get their attention or make a specific point. Maybe I've disagreed with their call or I'm trying to get them to look at something. I've got only a few seconds before the next play to plead my case. In those situations the most important thing to remember is to keep the focus on the decision and to not make it personal. Keep it on a professional level. You have to be careful in these situations: You want people to listen to the point you're making, not dismiss it because of the way you're making it. If I'm trying to point out to an official that a defensive lineman is continually holding my player, I want him to look for that, not get angry at me for screaming at him. I've had officials ignore me because of the way I've made my point, not because it isn't right. That's human nature. It's easy to write down this advice, but it's hard to remember in the moment. There is a tremendous amount of emotion surging through everybody on the field; there's joy and anger, and there's a lot of frustration, and it can change in an instant. My point is that we have to find ways to communicate with people whose goals and concerns are different from ours. One thing I do know for certain, though, is that shouting loudly is not particularly effective. There's no gain. It's difficult to present a rational argument when you're screaming. And in some instances screaming at the officials may have hurt my case.

Many veteran officials have been in the league for almost as long as I have. We know each other, and they've worked many games I've coached. As a group I respect them and believe they do a good job often under very difficult circumstances. That said, there are times when we don't see the game the same way. When that happens I try to help them, even when they don't want that help.

I do talk to the officials on the field. Every coach does. Does it help? Maybe. During Super Bowl XVII, for example, after we were called for holding, referee John Parry came over to the sideline and asked me if there was anything I wanted to discuss. I said, "John, we're trying to win a Super Bowl here. You can't make a holding call like that on Kevin Boothe."

"First of all," he said. "It wasn't me. But I'll go and check it out." A few plays later he came back. The official who made the call had spoken to the player who supposedly had been held. "He said it wasn't a good call," Parry told me. "But he wasn't going to complain about it, because it made up for all the calls he'd never gotten!"

There are times when anger is an appropriate response. At times I still get angry on the sidelines. I guess I always will. Players want their coach to be fighting for them, especially when they believe a bad call has been made. Sometimes expressing that is the right thing to do. It ignites passion. You have to show that winning makes a huge difference to you and that you're willing to fight for it. You have to show the people around you that you care enough to fight for them. I've never lost my passion for winning, so I'm never going to be able to completely contain my frustration on the sidelines. I'm never going to be calm and relaxed. The important thing is to maintain enough self-control to know when to express yourself and when to try to contain it. I have made an effort to tone it down at least a little bit, and Judy tells me that I do exercise at least a little more control.

MAKE CHANGES WHEN IT IS NECESSARY—BUT STICK TO YOUR CORE VALUES

Kurt Warner's list made it very clear that I had to improve my relationship with our players, but the reality is, I finally did it because I had to. I did it because my job was in jeopardy. Going into the 2007 season I had a year left on my original contract with the Giants. Our ownership suggested strongly that I try to improve my working relationship with our players and others suggested the same about my relationship with the media who covers the team. Trying to figure out how to do that, I asked several people I respected for advice. One of them was Charles Way, a former Giants player who had become the team's director of player development in 2000. Charles is the liaison between the coaching staff and the players. But he had also gone to college with my son Tim so he had seen me with my family, away from the football environment. He knew that at home I was a very different person. "Don't change your core values," he said, "because you need that discipline and that structure with today's player. But right now the players feel it's them against the coaching staff, that you don't care about them. So if you want them to play for you, you have to show them that you're sensitive to them, that you care about them. I know you do, but you have to show it to them."

Loosen up, he told me. Unbutton the top button of your

collar, and finally he said, in these words, "Let the players see you the way you are with your grandchildren." That suggestion had a huge impact on me. I thought about it when he said it, I thought about it driving home, I thought about it the next morning, and I thought it about before my next meeting with him. He was right; I was a different person with my family and friends than I was with my team. I had built and maintained an emotional curtain between myself and my players because I believed it helped maintain respect. And maybe it had at one time, but I was a dinosaur, and if I was going to survive I had to adapt. In the time I had been in the NFL, both as an assistant and a head coach, the game, the mentality, and the people who play the game had changed. Our society had changed. But I hadn't. The problem was that it was difficult for me to adapt and adjust to the changes that had taken place all around me without changing my core values.

I understood what Charles really meant: I had to allow my players to see that I was a human being, that I was a lot more compassionate than they had seen. The truth is that I did care about my players, I cared about them tremendously; I just didn't allow myself to show it very often.

The willingness and the ability to change is essential. That doesn't mean changing with the tides, going in and out all the time. You have to establish your principles and stick to them while also finding a way of making what you do relevant to the people you're working with. You can't expect to succeed by doing the same things the same way when the world around you is changing. I had to learn that. The first thing I had to do was to let my players know that I was aware of the problem and that I intended to change. To everyone's surprise, we scheduled a casino night in the stadium during our preseason minicamp. It's fair to say that the players didn't quite know how to react to that. What did it mean? The message that things were changing was reinforced one night during training camp. Instead of the scheduled team meeting, 120 of us got on buses and went bowling. That was absolutely the last thing any of my players could have anticipated. They couldn't figure out what was going on. Bowling? We're going bowling? With Coach Coughlin? The purpose was not to see who was the best bowler but to send a message: Things were going to change. The players laughed and hooted when I threw a gutter ball. Breaking the routine made the point that things were going to be very different—and showing it was much stronger than anything I could have said. It was so out of character for me but it was obvious to my players that something was changing. There was no question they got my message: I had gotten their message.

It's accurate to say that we have changed the working environment. But I haven't changed my core values, I haven't changed my coaching philosophy, I didn't change my personality, and we haven't changed our core culture. Everything we do emphasizes teamwork, hard work, and attention to detail. But what did change was that I found a better way to communicate with my team, a better way to express myself, and I adapted to the changes in the environment around me. Those changes made a big difference. The result was Michael Strahan saying several years later, "When Tom Coughlin got here I hated him. I wanted to play for anybody else but him. And now I would not want to play for anybody but him."

LEARN TO LISTEN

The other important lesson that I learned at that time is that positive communication requires that you listen to other people. Not just hear them, but actually listen to what they have to say, and pay attention to it. In addition to Charles Way, I met with Pat Hanlon, the Giants' senior vice president of communications. It would be accurate to say that at that time my relationship with the New York media was awful. The relationship between a leader who wants to control the flow of information about his team or company and the people whose job it is to report some things that, at best, aren't helpful for that leader, is always going to be difficult. The New York media thought I was rude, dismissive, surly, unpleasant, uncooperative, abrasive, and fill in whatever other adjectives you'd like to describe a combative, confrontational relation-ship. My wife looked right into my eyes and told me bluntly, "Tom, the media doesn't just dislike you. They hate you. So I'm telling you right now: Do something to help yourself."

To quote the classic line from the movie *Cool Hand Luke*, "What we have here is a failure to communicate." The Giants are a very public organization, and we have a large and extremely loyal fan base. My combative relationship with re-porters who covered the team made my job tougher and their job tougher. And I was the only one who could change that. Pat suggested that I meet individually with the dozen or so reporters who regularly covered the Giants. We set no ground rules for these meetings. We told the reporters that this was their opportunity to look me right in the eye and clear the air, that they should be honest and open about their issues with me, and we assured them that there would be absolutely no repercussions. I said, "You go ahead and tell me what you don't like about me, I'll tell you what I don't like about you, and we'll see if we can find some middle ground." We met in my office. Some of those meetings were brief, oth-ers lasted more than an hour. They were all cordial.

One-on-one I found that some people don't say the same things to your face that they'd said to others, or written, while others are quite candid. No one called me any names or explained why they'd written I should be fired. Mostly they told me they felt I had no understanding of their job, and that by being acerbic or evasive I was making that job more difficult. A columnist told me, "You act as if you don't have time for us." When I thought about that I realized that he was probably right. At times press conferences would go on for a long time, and after we had lost a football game, the last thing I wanted to do was sit there answering questions that I'd answered several times, or questions that I thought were ridiculous. When those things happened I wouldn't respond very well, or even very nicely. But after I heard that complaint, I knew I could do better than I was doing to help them do the best job possible.

Among the people I met with was *Newsday*'s Neil Best, who described the same problem from his viewpoint: "The men who had sat in that chair before Tom Coughlin had been the ultimate dream for a reporter in terms of accessibility," he said. "It was a rocky transition. He came in and lived up to his image as a tough guy with somewhat arbitrary rules. In training camp I asked an innocuous question and he snapped at me like he had no patience for it. And when he was giving one-word answers and being grouchy in his press conferences, we'd roll our eyes. It was not a good relationship.

"I went in there at six in the morning, and we met for an hour and a half. He didn't just sit there and listen; he seemed open to what I had to say and took copious notes. We had a discussion. He agreed with me on some points and contested other points. Most of what I said to him seemed fairly obvious. I told him that this was a lot simpler than he was making it. No one had an agenda against him, which he seemed to think there might be. We were just trying to do the best possible job, so when he gave us a hard time it didn't help us accomplish that.

"I even suggested that little things like saying our name when he answered a question, acknowledging us, might actually be an easy way to our hearts. So at the Super Bowl at the end of the year, when he started calling on the New York reporters by name I thought, wow, maybe he really was listening.

"Looking back on that situation, he hasn't changed fundamentally. He's the same person he was, but there now is a good level of mutual respect. Because of his consistency and integrity and the fact that he doesn't play favorites, I think he has grudgingly won the respect of the New York media in a way that I don't think any of us envisioned when it started."

The first thing I had to try was more patience. Patience had never been one of my strongest virtues. I have always been in a hurry, even when I wasn't quite certain where I was going. When I wanted something done, I wanted it done right away. If it wasn't, I didn't respond well. That wasn't a secret either. When we were moving into our new stadium in the Meadowlands, for example, there was the potential for all types of challenges. I told the coaching staff, "This isn't going to be seamless, so I want everybody to take his patience pills. Don't go off the handle, go with the flow, just be patient."

Me telling other people to be patient? Well, that got their attention. When I walked into our staff meeting the next day, I found that Chris Palmer, the quarterbacks' coach, had placed a container labeled PATIENCE PILLS in large letters and full of jelly beans on the table next to my chair. Without a word I reached into the jar, took out a handful, and swallowed them. Obviously, I had gotten that message.

I spent time reviewing my notes after these meetings with the reporters and figuring out what to do. I came away with a much greater understanding of how I was making it harder for them to get their job done. That was never my intention. I understand people taking pride in their work and wanting to do the best job they possibly can. I got that. And, as they explained to me, I was making it difficult for them. To do their job they needed my cooperation. One result of these meetings was that I promised myself that I'd at least pause and actually think about what I was about to say before responding to a reporter's question. I'd show some patience. I also came away with the realization that the people who communicated the best were people who did it with humor—and the very important knowledge that to communicate my thoughts I had to learn how to listen.

You can't communicate effectively if you don't listen. It's

that simple. At our team meetings, for example, I would stand in front of the room and make all the points I needed to make. Boom, boom, boom, boom, boom. I thought I was pretty clear about it, but later I would find out that there might be as many as five completely different interpretations of what I had just said. Different people heard the same words differently. Perhaps they heard what they wanted to hear. But it became obvious to me that no matter how well I thought I was making my point, if that many people got it wrong, I was not communicating effectively. I was just talking. I had to figure out how to do a better job.

To deal with that we formed what we called a Leadership Council consisting of ten players from all the position groups. The sole reason I did that was to improve the level of communication within our team. I wanted to make sure that the players were getting the information they needed. If there was any confusion, the members of the Leadership Council cleared it up. Rather than having to deal with fifty-three different players, I met with this smaller group regularly. In these meetings we would go over our upcoming schedule and discuss any issues or problems we were facing. I wanted the team to have plenty of notice of what we intended to do, and when we intended to do it, to give players and their families the chance to make their own plans. I also wanted to make sure that we were all on the same page, that everybody understood precisely what I was saying. I gave these leaders real responsibility, allowing them to take care of issues that in the past would have ended up on my desk, without my having to get involved.

I did one other thing. I not only listened to the Leadership Council, I paid attention to their requests. For example, in my twelve years as a head coach in the NFL, I'd never had permanent captains. The Leadership Council voted unanimously that we should have three season-long captains. We did, and those three captains added an extra layer of leadership that helped keep the team together throughout the season. When we were preparing for Super Bowl XLII, instead of simply announcing what the curfew would be, as I would have done in the past, we discussed it. We agreed that early in the week there would be no curfew, but we would institute a curfew as the week progressed. We got total buy-in from the team. The players understood that they had a stake in the decision-making process. As All-Pro lineman Chris Snee, who is also my son-in-law, said about me that season, "He tweaked a few things. He's established a better relationship with the players. Now he'll hear both sides of an argument."

I have changed. I'm certainly not as rigid as I once was. I don't want to be perceived as a stuffed shirt. Maybe I'll stand in front of the team at a meeting and do some jumping jacks. The players love it—they may think I'm a little nuts, but they love it. Now I try to be less predictable, to shake their preconceptions. We played the Cowboys on New Year's Day 2012, and at the end of our team meeting on New Year's Eve, we opened the doors and waiters walked in, carrying champagne for everyone. Everyone was shocked. Tom Coughlin serving champagne to his team the night before a game? "You spend New Year's Eve with your family," I told them, "and this is our family."

ESTABLISH TRUST

Change is hard to institute. When we introduced these changes there were a lot of people who were skeptical that it was anything more than a temporary Band-Aid. I suspect they were afraid that anything they said to me during this period of candor might come back to bite them when I returned to my old ways. Getting people to talk honestly to their boss requires that you establish a level of trust, and it takes time to build that trust. In any business situation, including a football team, there are always people who will tell the boss what they believe he wants to hear rather than saying what they really believe. My friend Dick Jauron likes to tell a wonderful story that exemplifies this attitude. It took place when he was my defensive coordinator at Jacksonville. As he tells it, "We weren't having a very good day defensively. Our offense would score, and then the other team would come right back and score. We were losing by a few points in the fourth quarter. So after we scored, I heard Tom's voice in my headphones asking me, 'If we onside kick and don't recover the ball, will we stop them?'

"When the head coach asks you that there is only one answer. And it isn't, 'No, we can't stop them.' So I told him, 'You kidding me? Sure we'll stop them.' We tried an onside kick; they recovered it and moved right down the field and scored. Then, sure enough, we went right back the other way and scored. Once again, there was Tom's voice in my ear, asking the same question, 'Will we stop them if we onside kick?' I thought the answer was pretty clear by then. What I wanted to say was, 'Coach, we haven't stopped them yet.' Instead, I told him what I thought he wanted to hear, 'Go ahead. Onside kick and we'll stop them.'

"'Well, we haven't stopped them yet!'"

Putting anyone in a position in which they feel compelled to tell you what they think you want to hear doesn't work. It hurts rather than helps you reach your goal. The way to change that is by listening to what people say and then taking action based on their suggestions. And when they're wrong, as everyone will be at some point, you don't turn around and blame them. Sometimes you have to demonstrate to people that you hear what they have to say even if what they are saying isn't what you want to hear. Figuratively and, at least in one example, literally. At our Saturday night team meeting before a Sunday game, if we've won the week before, we play a highlight reel showing our people making great plays. It's a "rock 'em, sock 'em, go get 'em, here's what we're going to do tomorrow" tape. We always add an upbeat musical soundtrack to this tape, something to communicate a message. I'm not a huge fan of rap or heavy metal. Sometimes I don't understand a word of it. But, as I've learned, that music isn't meant to please me or get me ready to play. The players' taste picks the music. If that's the type of music that starts their engines, that's what we play.

I've become more tolerant. When I look back at things that I did in the past, there are certain decisions I wouldn't make today. For example, when I was at Jacksonville, two rookies racing to get to a Saturday night meeting in the rain went speeding over a bridge and got into an accident. It was a fender bender, and fortunately nobody was hurt. But it made those players late for the meeting. This had been a continuing problem with them, and they'd been warned several times. I was angry, and I fined them, not for being in a car accident but for not giving themselves sufficient time to get to work on time. When the media found out about it, they wrote that I had fined players for being late because they were in an accident. That was not true, and it certainly wasn't the message I wanted to communicate. If that same situation occurred today, I wouldn't fine those players. In that situation, fining them sent the wrong message.

BE DIRECT

Through the years I've developed my own methods for communicating effectively with my staff and my team. It's a pretty simple rule: When I have something to say, I say it. I don't waste time looking for the politically correct way to make my point. I am blunt without being rude. I can do that because everybody knows that my goal is the same as theirs: Win. That's already established. So whatever I say is meant to help us reach that goal as a team. It is never meant to be personal. As a result, as tight end Bear Pascoe told a reporter in 2011, "He's always straight up with us. He tells us what he's thinking. We know where he stands." Steve Spagnuolo said the same thing: "You're going to know exactly where you stand with Tom Coughlin, because he's going to let you know."

I don't waste time, my time or the time of those people I work with. When I schedule a meeting, it starts on Coughlin Time, and every aspect of it is planned, even to the moment when an assistant is supposed to dim the lights. Before the meeting I've prepared or approved just about every word that is going to be said to my team. When I'm speaking to the team almost nothing is spontaneous, and I don't allow anyone else to speak without my approval. Every word, every piece of footage, is consistent with the theme we are trying to implement. Every speaker we invite to address the team, every sign we hang in the locker room, everything we give them to read has been chosen because it reinforces the concept we are trying to communicate.

John Wooden always believed that people learn more effectively if they are given smaller bites of information each time rather than being served the whole information meal. Rather than having a general rule like that, I think it's important to understand how much information each person can comprehend and give them as much as they can assimilate. We try to give each player the information he needs to succeed, and then work with him to make sure he understands it, digests it, and can apply it on the field. Part of each assistant coach's job is knowing just how much information his players can absorb. You have to know the physical and mental capabilities of your people and work within the range of what's possible. We follow this principle (from Confucius) in our teaching: "I hear and I forget. I see and I remember. I do and I understand." We use a variety of teaching methods to communicate to people: lectures, video/Powerpoint, demonstrations, jog-throughs, and testing. We work with the entire team, with various units, and on an individual basis. And we keep working until we're confident that we've successfully communicated the message.

I'm also a sticky note guy. Where other people might send an e-mail, I'll write on a Post-it. There's nothing more direct than a simple message waiting for someone when he walks into the office. It's not one of a long list of e-mails; it's the first thing they see. The fact that I took the time to write it and put it right in front of him or her makes it clear that this is a priority. Pay attention to this. Get it done. When I do give a note or a project to an assistant, it is his duty to follow up to the point when it is completely carried out, without questioning it. So I'm constantly writing little notes and leaving them where I know they'll be found. I'm as direct on these notes as I am in person. Generally they cover those thousand little details I've noticed and want taken care of right away: The light's out in my office and I need a new bulb. The grand catchall: See me. Every assistant knows when they walk into their office and finds one of my notes that it is something that needs to be taken care of right away.

Very often, when members of our coaching staff arrive in the morning, they'll find a note stuck to their desk. For me it's a way of reminding people that details matter. In 2002, I hired Mike Priefer, a graduate of the Naval Academy, as the Jaguars' assistant special teams coach and my scheduling assistant. As he tells the story, he had made some small mistake on the schedule, and when he came into work the following morning he found a note on his master schedule reading, "This is not what I expect from you. This is not what I expect from a Naval Academy graduate. It is not what I expect from one of my assistant coaches."

He later said, "I kept that sticky note with me the entire season to remind me that there's no time for amateur hour in the NFL. That note taught me that everyone in the NFL, even the lowest guy on the totem poll like I was, has details he has to focus on, that mistakes cannot be tolerated."

Sometimes, as I learned, earning the right to win requires taking a hard and honest look at the way you're doing things and admitting that you have to make changes. My message hasn't changed, but the way I communicate it has. And that has made a significant difference, both in my effectiveness as a coach and the quality of our working environment—which translates into winning.

FIVE

Motivation

When men put all of their energies into something that is greater than themselves, they forge a bond that will last a lifetime.

—Colonel Greg Gadson

A leader's job is to motivate his people to give their best possible effort all the time. Dan Edwards, our vice president for communications at Jacksonville, once said, "Every great coach always believes his team is going to win. The real job is to convince his team that they're good enough to win. "

PRIDE IS THE FOUNDATION OF MOTIVATION

Motivation is the emotional tool used to get a team, and every individual on it, focused and playing to the best of their ability. It's the job of a coach, manager, or supervisor in any area to figure out how to accomplish that. There isn't any secret, and what works for one team or person may not work at all for others. There is a general perception among sports fans, among football fans in particular, that motivation consists of a coach like Knute Rockne making an extraordinary locker room speech before sending his troops onto the field, his voice rising to a crescendo as he urges his team to "win one for the Gipper." And then they charge out of the locker room bursting with determination.

Well, it doesn't really work that way. That is not the way it happens in the NFL. Or in the corporate world. Maybe years ago coaches would make that type of inspirational speech, and even today there might well be some shouting in the locker room at halftime if a team hasn't played well. But motivation is an art and an instinct. I've read the words of masters. "Pride is a much better motivator than fear," wrote John Wooden. "It produces far better results that last for a much longer time." President Eisenhower, who planned the D-Day invasion, said, "Motivation is the art of getting people to do what you want them to do because they want to do it." And I've been learning how to do it for longer than four decades. I've learned from my experiences what works for me.

As a leader you can motivate your entire team as a single unit or you can motivate your people individually—and to some degree there is an overlap—but in both cases the very first thing you have to do is build pride: pride in the team and individual pride. When I came home after a high school football game and my father criticized me for giving less than my best effort, he was appealing to my pride. The lesson that he taught me in so many ways is that pride is not given to you; it's something you earn. My entire self-esteem was built on my belief that I was working to the best of my ability, and when he pointed out that I wasn't really doing that, that maybe I was skating by a little, my pride was hurt.

Pride in yourself is what motivates you to keep going at the end of the game, when you think you don't have anything left in your tank. It's what keeps you at the office late at night to put the final touches on a project, little things that only you might notice. NFL players are the best in the world at what they do, and we want them to take pride in their ability and their accomplishments. Self-pride is the engine of the self-starter. The simple phrase, You can do better than that, spoken by someone you respect, is about as good a motivational tool as has ever been discovered. No one has ever described the value of self-pride as a motivational tool better than Michael Strahan when he said, "My greatest motivation was the fear of failure. I knew the team was depending on me, and the very last thing I wanted to do was let my teammates down."

Everywhere I've coached, my rules have been designed to build a sense of pride in the team, to reinforce the message that we are all in this battle together. The rules apply to everyone equally. We remind them every day that they are good enough to be part of what we believe is the greatest organization in professional sports. We take pride in our professional appearance at all times, we all wear New York Giants issued clothing and use Giants equipment. If one does it, everybody does it. I've always discouraged any display of individualism, because our focus is on pride in the team. At our facility, the Timex Performance Center in the Meadowlands, everywhere you turn you'll see that big blue NY logo on a wall or a piece of clothing, or huge photographs of the great Giants players. You'll see the four Super Bowl trophies the organization has won displayed as soon as you walk in the front door. We want our people to understand that they are privileged to have joined an organization with a long and proud tradition, a great history, and a tremendously loyal fan base. And while they reap the benefits of that simply by wearing a Giants uniform, it also means they have an obligation to live up to the standards set by all those people who came before them. I emphasize to everyone in our organization that they never take that NY off. No matter where they go, whatever they do, they will be identified first as a New York Giant. "You're a Giant twenty-four/seven," I emphasize. "The name never comes off. So whatever you do doesn't just reflect on you, it reflects on this entire organization." We have always emphasized to our players that that NY on their helmet is a lot more important than their name on the back.

The first thing I've done wherever I've coached is begin trying to build pride in our organization, and at each place, I've done it a different way. At RIT I emphasized how fortunate my players were to be members of the team that was responsible for making the transition from club football to the Independent Collegiate Athletic Conference. They were the first representatives of a wonderful university to do so, and it was their responsibility to build a tradition for the people who would follow them. I got the university to allow us to move our games from a beaten-up practice football field to the gorgeous soccer field, and I worked with the crew in laying down the lines on that field. We worked hard at it, because it was important that our field and appearance be first class. When we were done, that field was as perfect as it was possible to make it, every hash mark was straight and in the right place, because I wanted our players to take pride in it. I wanted them to see that everything we did, we did with pride, and to understand that everything we did we were going to do to the best of our abilities. Within three seasons we were competing against the best teams in Division III, and all these years later those players still take great pride in their accomplishments.

At Boston College we instituted a very tough training

program. The team worked out at 6:00 A.M. three times a week, not simply to build muscle and stamina, but to build pride in being a member of the team. These people were suffering together, for the team, and they took great pride in their ability to survive it. It definitely brought the team together. We started the 1993 season 0–2, then won seven straight games. In mid-November we traveled to South Bend, Indiana, to meet undefeated and number-one ranked Notre Dame. A week earlier the Irish had earned the top ranking by defeating the then number-one Florida State Seminoles in what had been called the "game of the century." This was the game after the "game of the century." Few people gave us much of a chance, but we had spent the entire season building our confidence. In four previous meetings we'd never beaten Notre Dame, but in that game, we never backed down, eventually winning 41–39. Then we beat the University of Virginia 31–13 in the Carquest Bowl. Those BC players also continue to take tremendous pride in their accomplishments.

Even in the NFL, where players earn millions of dollars, pride is still an extremely strong motivator. The money is important, obviously; professional football is a business. But once a player signs on the dotted line, it stops being about the money. It's about being able to wear that Super Bowl championship ring. It's about people looking at you and members of

your family with respect, because you are a champion. I tell
my teams over and over that professionally there is no greater
feeling in the world than to win a world championship. The
satisfaction and the pride that comes with that win is greater
than anything you can imagine. I tell them that for the rest of
their lives the one question that I guarantee they are going to
be asked is, How many championships did you win? People
talk about the fact that Marv Levy's great Buffalo Bills teams
did not win four consecutive Super Bowls, not that the Bills
achieved the extraordinary feat of getting into four consecutive Super Bowls. Pride is derived from being recognized as
the best at whatever you do. Not the second best.

From the day I tramped my muddy feet into our trailer in
Jacksonville we emphasized to every single person working
for that franchise—even when we were a football team without any football players—that it was our responsibility to
build a winning tradition for the city. At my very first press
conference in New York I told the media that my objective
was to restore New York Giants' pride. The Giants were one
of the original NFL franchises and had a long and very proud
history. The Giants–Baltimore Colts 1958 championship game
that the Colts won in overtime is still considered one of the
greatest games in football history and is at least partially responsible for the tremendous growth of the league. Great
players like Frank Gifford, Phil Simms, and Lawrence Taylor
had been Giants. Head coach Bill Parcells brought me to

New York to coach wide receivers in 1988, and in 1990 we'd beaten the Buffalo Bills in the famous "wide right" game to win Super Bowl XXV. But by the time I was hired in 2004, the team had lost some of that luster and had finished 4–12 the previous year. The pride in being a New York Giant that had been so much a part of the organization when I had worked for Coach Parcells was missing. Everything we did from that first press conference on was intended to restore that pride.

During the 2011 season, former Giant Phil Simms was broadcasting our game against Buffalo. We'd lost to Seattle the week before and hadn't played well. Simms had been a great quarterback who had led the Giants to victory in Super Bowl XXI. During the week I asked if he would speak to the team. Although he had been retired for almost two decades, his message was about the pride he still felt about having been a New York Giant. "I will always be a Giant," he told them. "I am proud to be a Giant. It is an honor to be part of the greatest organization in football." You really could feel the pride as he spoke.

Later in that season we had a difficult situation with defensive end Justin Tuck. Justin had started every game for us for the previous four seasons and been very productive, averaging just about ten sacks a year. But in 2011 he was banged-up physically and mentally. He had missed four games with injuries to his neck, groin, toe, shoulder, and ankle and played at less than full strength in others. During that same period, both his grandfather and his uncle, with whom he was very close, had died. Justin was one of our captains, and we needed him to be playing to the best of his ability. But he was walking around the locker room with his head down, as if all the joy had been drained out of him. It was obvious he had begun to doubt himself. As he admitted to reporters, "I'm not me. I'm not. There are days I sit here and mope around, talking about how I [stink]. . . . There are some weeks when I don't feel like I'm helping the football team. I don't think we've lost any faith, but it's tough to go in every day and say my hard work is going to pay off. . . . I just feel as though that sometimes I'm doing more harm being on the field some weeks than me being off it."

After we'd been beaten by New Orleans in late November, I asked Justin to come see me. All his injuries and his frustrations seemed to have come to a head during that game. He wasn't playing anywhere near his capabilities. If we had any hope of making the play-offs, we needed a fully committed Justin Tuck. We sat in my office, and we talked like a father and son, rather than a coach and a player, about what was going on in his life. Basically, I appealed to his pride. Justin is a very proud man, both in what he has accomplished as an individual and what the team has accomplished. We needed him, I told him, and he wasn't responding. "You're letting things that shouldn't have control over you dominate your life, rather than the other way around. You're bigger than all of this, you're better than that. You have so much to give to your teammates. You've had the greatest training; you were in the same meeting room with Michael Strahan when you were just a rookie. You learned from him. Now you've got teammates who are starving to get that same knowledge from you. Starving to hear your message and see the real you. The excited you, the guy with the big heart and the tremendous spirit. And they're not getting it. What happens now is up to you, you're the only one who came make this decision."

Every word I said to him was true. That was essential. An individual like Justin Tuck is too smart to believe anything less than the absolute truth. You can't motivate someone by exaggerating their capabilities. He knew I wasn't blowing smoke; I wasn't trying to pump up his ego. I was asking him to stop feeling sorry for himself and take a harsh look at reality. He was not performing to the best of his ability. I was appealing to his pride, knowing real motivation comes from inside. He understood he was letting down his teammates, but probably more important, he also knew he was letting himself down. All I did was force him to deal with that.

His pride kicked in. He made the decision that he was ready to play to the level of his talent. He came back strong for the remainder of the season. He didn't just raise his level of his play; other players told him that just by being out on the field and playing his best, he raised their level of play. He led the defense in our Super Bowl victory with two sacks of Tom Brady. "Planting himself firmly," as a reporter wrote, "in the storied annals of the New York Giants history."

Years from now, when other New York Giants players are struggling with injuries or other issues, they'll have the example set by Justin Tuck to draw on—just as he was able to draw on the standard set by players before him. Pride in your organization and pride in your own contribution to the success of that organization makes a tremendous difference in everything from your work ethic in the off-season to your play in the last few minutes of the fourth quarter of a game in the freezing cold in December.

Everybody wants to be part of a winning organization, in business as well as in sports. Everybody wants the work they do to have meaning to the entire organization. Most jobs aren't glamorous, and most people don't have eighty thousand fans rooting for them, so it's up to management to remind them at every opportunity of their importance to the entire organization. The pride we take in the Giants organization isn't limited to the players and coaches. We want every person, from the receptionist who greets people when they walk in the door to the people working in food preparation to know that they all play an important role in our success. We want them to enjoy the praise they get when people hear they work for the New York Giants. Everybody in the organization has to know that his or her contribution to our success is recognized and appreciated.

POSITIVE AND NEGATIVE MOTIVATION

I am relentless in driving people to be the best they can be. I push my coaching staff to hold their players to the highest expectations. And I expect them to use every means possible to insure that will happen. This means that every coach is faced with the challenge of motivating his people. While positive is always preferable, in some situations negative motivation will work, too, at least for a short period of time. New York Yankees' owner George Steinbrenner, who became renowned for criticizing his players and staff, once admitted, "They say I'm tough to work for. Well, I am. But I'm not trying to win any popularity contest. I know only one way and that is to work my butt off and demand everybody else do the same."

People will play for their job when it's threatened. As Lou Holtz, who led Notre Dame to nine consecutive bowl games and the 1988 national championship, once said, "Motivation is simple. You eliminate those who are not motivated." Even John Wooden said, "The best motivation is the bench." People will do what they have to do to succeed. That's instinctive. Personally, though, I haven't found "or else" to be a lasting motivational tool. While at times it works, and fear motivates people to improve their performance, it certainly doesn't help encourage teamwork. If you're too critical too often of a person you have to work with, eventually you're going to lose the ability to communicate with them. When they see you coming, they're going to turn around and go in the other direction. I've always felt it's better to build a bridge rather than tear one down. You just might need that bridge later.

Positive reinforcement can be a strong motivational tool if a good relationship exists between coaches and players or any type of supervisor and the people he or she supervises. It's human nature: People want to please those they respect, because they want to be respected in return. When I was in high school I worked as hard as I did in football practice because I didn't want to let my coaches down. I admired them so much, I wanted to earn their praise. There is no better reinforcement than a compliment. Just a few words of praise—"Nice job, way to go"—coming from a person you respect can carry tremendous weight. It can make you want to bust through a wall if that's what it takes to earn that praise. Just imagine how it must feel to come out of a game and having a demanding coach like Wooden, Lombardi, Bill Parcells, Tom Landry, Bob Knight, or any of the other legendary disciplinarians waiting there to compliment you for doing a good job. Those are the memories that never fade. One of the proudest memories I have of my career is Doug Flutie telling a reporter, "I studied hard because I didn't want to make a mental mistake. I didn't want to let Coach Coughlin down."

The night before we played the Jets in October 2007, rookie Aaron Ross broke a team rule. He admitted it and apologized, but he was fined and benched for the first half of the game. It's fair to say he accepted the penalty, but he was not happy with me. His pride was hurt. When he went into the game at the beginning of the second half, he had something to prove. In the final eight minutes of the game he intercepted two passes; the first one prevented a touchdown and the second one he ran in for a touchdown. When he came off the field I went right over to him and screamed over the crowd, "Great job!"

"Thanks, Coach," he said. Then we embraced. That is about as good an example as possible of the benefits of both positive and negative motivation. He had earned both the punishment and the praise, and having paid a penalty and sat on the bench, those few words of praise that he had earned with his play made a big difference. The penalty had made him want to prove me wrong; the praise made him want to perform even better.

I've always been honest with my players about their performance. They expect that from me. I've never hesitated to be critical when a player deserved it, but I've also always made it clear that my objective wasn't to blame anyone, but rather to correct the mistake and do everything possible to make sure it never happens again. The way we phrase it is, "Fix the problem, not the blame." But because I can be critical, when I praise someone they know I mean it. They know they've earned that praise.

If you are going to be critical, you also have to make absolutely sure that you find a way to offer praise. I never praise anyone in anticipation of performance. A compliment isn't a treat; it's a reward. Praise is earned through performance. When it is earned I make sure to deliver it. That's why, in addition to praising players who have earned it as they come off the field, we always show video highlights of the best plays of the week to the whole team. We want the whole team to know that this player did a great job. We want players to feel the warmth of their teammates' respect, because we want them to enjoy that feeling so much that they're going to go out the next week and perform on that same level again. At the same time that we're praising an individual's performance, we're reinforcing the concept that his play contributed to the team's success, and that his effort for the team is appreciated by his teammates. For us, everything we do is for the benefit of the team.

DEVELOP A THEME

The objective is to get the entire team moving together toward your goal: to win. There are a lot of steps on the road to victory, and each one may be different and require a different approach. The long-term goal never changes, but you have to take each step independently. I'm a big believer in using themes as a motivational tool, both long-term, big themes and weekly themes. A theme is nothing more than a concept that identifies who you are and what you want to accomplish. In business, some companies can be recognized immediately by their themes: "we try harder"; "the friendly skies." Other themes have become legendary to sports fans: "We're number one!" "Ya gotta believe!" "Threepeat!" A theme has to be brief, clear, and concise, a rallying cry that every member of the team can buy into. A few words that symbolize who you are. That first season in Jacksonville, when we were building an organizational culture, our theme was pride: Feel pride, build pride.

The Giants theme for the 2011 season was one word: "Finish." It was what we didn't do in 2010. Midway through that

2010 season we were 6–2, but we had difficulty holding onto leads the whole year. We played Philadelphia with three weeks left in the season for a spot in the play-offs. We led 24–3 at half-time; we led the game 31–10 with 8:17 left. It seemed like an insurmountable lead. But the Eagles scored twenty-eight points in the final 7:18, the game-winning points coming with 13 seconds left, on the first and only game-winning punt return for a touchdown in NFL history. After that game, I admitted, "I've never been around anything like this in my life. It's about as empty as you get to feel in this business, right there."

We ended the 2010 season in a first-place tie with the Eagles, at 10–6, but because they had beaten us twice, they went to the play-offs and we went home. If we had played that late December game to the finish, played those last minutes the way we had been playing the first three and a half quarters, I'm convinced we would have had an opportunity to go to the Super Bowl. But we didn't finish. That was a terrible winter for me. I spent the entire off-season wondering what we could have done differently. The first day of minicamp I announced that our theme for the year was going to be "finish." Finish what you start, no matter what it takes. Finish every play until the whistle blows; play in the fourth quarter like you were playing in the first quarter; don't stop until you cross the finish line.

To achieve our goal, to win, we had to finish. That became the dominant theme for the year. We printed it on T-shirts, we posted it on the wall in the locker room, and we used quotes that made that point. Finish! There wasn't a meeting or a practice or a speech the entire season where we failed to hit that theme.

Our assistant video director, Ed Triggs, was watching ESPN one weekend in the spring and came across a video that illustrated the point we wanted to make better than anything we could say. It was the story of the San Francisco University High School girls cross country team. Their coach, Jim Tracy, who'd led the team to seven state championships, had been diagnosed with ALS. The team was desperate to give him the gift of an eighth championship. In this video, Coach Tracy preaches the same message to his team that we were telling our team: "It's purely determination that allows you to finish," and "You need to finish; that's the point." In the state championship meet, the team's captain is seen staggering toward the finish line and collapsing only a few feet away. Remarkably, she crawled across the finish line to help her team win the championship. It was an unbelievable display of determination. We showed our players the story the very first day of training camp, and we showed it the week before the Super Bowl. We showed them the image of the young runner crossing the finish line when we played the Eagles in September—and sure enough, this time we won that game in the fourth quarter. We finished. And we showed that image again before our final game of the season, when we had to beat the Cowboys at Met Life Stadium to win the division championship. In that five-month period the story of Jim Tracy and his team had taken on an entirely new meaning, but it continued to reinforce our season-long theme: Finish.

We finished. At one point in mid-December, our record was 7–7, but we then won six straight games against the toughest teams in the NFL, to finish 13–7. In every one of those six games, including four play-off games, we outscored every opponent in the fourth quarter. And we finished the season by upsetting Tom Brady's New England Patriots in Super Bowl XLVI.

Another extremely effective theme we employed was our 2007 rallying cry, "road warriors." We opened that season by losing in Dallas, and then won eleven consecutive road games. Winning any game on the road in the NFL is difficult; winning eleven consecutive games on the road is amazing. That season we won more games on the road than we did at home. The "road warriors" theme wasn't a concept we planned; it grew out of our performance. After we'd started this streak, it took on its own meaning. The whole team bought into the theme; we took tremendous pride in our ability to win on the road. It became self-fulfilling. We began to believe we couldn't lose on the road, accepting the challenge as a test of our team character. The reality is that winning builds confidence which leads to more winning. It was amazing the way that team came together; everybody contributed and nobody was looking for individual credit. The expression I used to describe it was "the intangible feeling of unselfish commitment."

Very few teams have ever had a more difficult path to the Super Bowl than we did that season. After beating Tampa Bay in Florida, we beat the top-seeded Cowboys in Dallas, the Packers in a –24 degree wind chill in Green Bay, and finally the 18–0 Patriots in Glendale, Arizona. Our historic performance on the road will always be considered one of the most amazing winning streaks in league history.

In addition to our broad themes for the season, each week we introduce smaller themes, those things we want our players to focus on that week. Our weekly themes include goals like: "Run the ball, stop the run"; "Penalties lose games"; "Respect all, fear none"; "Humble enough to prepare, confident enough to perform"; "Get physical'; "Giants pride"; "Team first"; and "Your work ethic must exceed the expectation level." When we played that supposedly meaningless game against the Patriots in the final week of the 2007 regular season, our theme was "High energy, extreme focus, and great competition." I understand that the more of these you hang up on the wall, the less impact any single one of them might have, but together they reinforce confidence, positive think-ing, and good advice.

SUCCESS MOTIVATES SUCCESS

There aren't many better motivational tools than winning. When you win everything tastes better, there's less traffic, the sky is bluer, and the whole world is a better place to be. Win-ning in anything you do results in the same feeling, from a teacher finally breaking through to a student to a plumber finding the source of a leak or a manager leading his team to record-breaking sales numbers. There is a great feeling of ac-complishment when all the work you've done in practice, all the sacrifices you've made to get to that moment, and the losses you've suffered, culminate in a victory. I've been fortu-nate enough to have many memorable victories in my career, but few of them were more satisfying than the final game of our first season in Jacksonville in 1995. We had won three games earlier in the season, but then lost seven in a row. A week earlier we'd been blown out by the Lions, 44–0. It seemed like we were heading in the wrong direction. But that last game we beat Bill Belichick's Cleveland Browns in Jacksonville. It was an extremely important win for us, be-cause it was evidence we were on the right track after all. We went home feeling positive, knowing we'd struggled through some rough spots but that there was real hope that we would be a strong team in our second season. That one win provided great motivation heading into the off-season.

After we suffered what seemed to be an unusually high number of injuries in 2011, we adopted the secondary theme, "No toughness, no championship." That particular theme proved to be personally painful to me. We drilled that idea into our players: be tough, play with pain, the toughest team is going to be there at the finish. On Christmas Eve we were playing the Jets in another must-win game. We were leading in the fourth quarter when our running back, D. J. Ware, got shoved out of bounds on our 42-yard line—right into my left leg. He slammed into me, literally tearing my hamstring from the bone. I got hit, but I never went down. Our medical team wanted to take me into the locker room, but I refused to go. After what we'd been preaching all season, showing weakness when the game was still on the line was absolutely the last thing I was going to do. I sat on the bench for one play, but the players were blocking my view of the field, so I stood back up on the sidelines. After we won the game, 29–14, I hobbled into the locker room. Every player who walked by me made a point of reminding me, with a smile, "no toughness, no championship."

The fact is, I loved that response. It was evidence to me

that the team had taken that theme to heart. My leg injury gave me the opportunity to prove to them that the themes applied to the entire organization, to the coaches and the people running our facility as well as to the players. We were all in. If they could play hurt, I certainly could coach hurt. I didn't miss a single snap.

RESPECT YOUR COMPETITION

There was another motivating factor in that game against the Jets. Every coach, including me, tells their players to be careful what they say to the media. There's just no reason to provoke your competition. Build them up in the media, compliment their achievements, but don't give them material to post on their bulletin board to get their people riled up. Your competition doesn't have to be bad for you to be better. So another one of our motivating themes during the 2007 season was, "Talk is cheap; play the game." We posted this theme on the wall, we wore it on T-shirts, and we focused on proving how good we were on the playing field, not talking about it.

As most people know, we share MetLife Stadium in the New Jersey Meadowlands with the New York Jets. The Christmas Eve game was a Jets home game, which gave them certain very minor advantages. On the stadium wall outside our locker room we had painted a mural depicting our Super Bowl victories. When our players arrived at the stadium that day they discovered that the Jets had placed a black curtain over the mural. Two of our players ripped down the curtain, but the Jets hung it right back up. It was a completely unnecessary provocation. I can't imagine that covering up a representation of your opponent's success is an effective motivational tool, but maybe it worked for them. I do know it worked for us. We didn't hesitate to point it out to our players before the game, reminding them that the Jets were attacking the accomplishments, the history, and the tradition of the New York Giants franchise. There was one thing we could do about it: We could win the game. And after we'd won it, our Pro Bowl offensive lineman, David Diehl, said, "This game was about respect. It was a lot more than just us, this team, and this year. It's about our organization, our history, our tradition. Walking in here today we knew we were the away team, but to have all our logos blocked, all the Super Bowl trophies this organization's won, and everything we stand for . . . We all saw it as a sign of disrespect." There is no question that the Jets' action provided an additional spark to get our engines ignited.

I never belittle an opponent. This is the NFL, the greatest professional sports league in existence. These are the best players in the world. It's an honor to be part of it. I've always believed it's more productive to build my team rather than tear down an opponent. Before we played top-seeded Dallas in their stadium for the 2007 NFC divisional play-off game, the Cowboys' owner, Jerry Jones, left two tickets for the following week's NFC title game on each of his player's stools. Maybe he believed that he was motivating the Cowboys, but we took it as an insult. To us his message was clear: He was so certain that the Cowboys were going to beat us that he was already handing out tickets for the championship game. We were just another game. Basically, he was dismissing us.

I didn't think that was necessary. And it turned out to be a better motivational tool for us than it was for the Cowboys. We were pretty angry about it. So in our locker room after we had beaten them, as the team gathered around me—and the media wrote down and filmed every word—I told them seriously, "I don't want anyone talking about this in the media, but . . ." and then I extended my arm high over my head as if I were holding something, smiled broadly, and yelled, "Jerry just sent the tickets over. So, we're all set." The players cheered in approval. They certainly had gotten the motivational message.

INSPIRATION FROM OUTSIDE

I believe in the motivational impact of meeting room speeches. They're not always the rah-rah type but they can be very moving. Every once in a while I invite someone very special to speak to the team. Almost always this will be someone who has lived the message he will be delivering, someone who will reinforce the values and principles we want to communicate to our players, someone who has earned the right to possess their attention. I don't do it too often, and only when I believe this is an individual who can inspire the team. These are not people who work in football, which reinforces my belief that the values that apply to living a successful life are the same values that lead to winning a professional football game. My players enjoy having these speakers from different worlds; it's definitely a way of attracting and keeping their attention. Generally these people speak to the team at our Saturday night meeting before a Sunday game. "The game plan has been set," is the way Eli Manning describes these meetings. "The preparation has been done. It's one last chance for some good thoughts, to make sure we're all on the same page and confident we're going to play well."

One of the most impactful speakers we've ever had is Colonel Greg Gadson. Colonel Gadson had played three seasons of varsity football at West Point before serving in America's recent wars. In May 2007, his vehicle was blown up by a roadside bomb in Baghdad, and he lost both legs. Within months he was testing the new type of powered prosthetic leg that lets people walk easily and with a natural step. Eventually, incredibly, he was even able to return to duty, and in June 2012 took command of Fort Belvoir in Virginia, becoming the first double amputee in history to command a major army installation.

But only four months after nearly losing his life and suffering a life-changing injury in Iraq, at the suggestion of Colonel Gadson's former teammate at West Point, our wide receivers' coach, Mike Sullivan, I invited him to speak to the team on the Saturday night before what was to become the most important game of our season. We had lost the first two games of the 2007 season and were traveling to Washington to play the Redskins, a division rival. Three losses to open the season in an extremely competitive division is a very deep hole to try to dig out of. As Colonel Gadson remembers, "I just spoke from the heart, as a soldier and as a former football player, for about ten or fifteen minutes. I talked to them about appreciating the opportunities in their lives, how special and privileged they were, how everybody needs to understand what they truly have. And I talked to them about the power of sports in people's lives, especially soldiers' lives.

"I told them that after all the exteriors had been stripped away, they played the game for themselves. But that they had to play the game for each other. Then I talked about myself, how my old teammates came to my need, and how I was reminded again of the power of a team, the emotional commitment teammates have for each other, that when a team finds a way to do things greater than they thought they could do, that they couldn't have done individually, that a bond is formed that can live forever . . . and how whatever they were going through at that point in the season that no success ever came easy. And finally I reminded them that nothing is promised to anybody in this life, starting with tomorrow."

It was a remarkable speech. It was so emotional that when he was done I just ended the meeting. I decided my prepared remarks were no longer necessary. If his words didn't motivate that team to play for each other, with an unselfish commitment to the team, there was nothing I or anyone else could do or say that would accomplish that. Anything else we did would just diminish the power of his speech. The next day we came back from a two-touchdown deficit to beat the Redskins, a game that ended with a four-down goal line stand that probably saved our season. That was the first of six straight wins and it was the beginning of the team's relationship with Colonel Gadson. He watched several of our games from the sidelines, including the NFC Championship Game in frigid Green Bay, where he served as our honorary cocaptain, and Super Bowl XLII. After our victory in Arizona we awarded him a Super Bowl ring as a member of our team for his motivational contribution.

In addition to Colonel Gadson, we have also been fortunate enough to have General Ray Odierno, chief of staff of the army, speak to the team on more than one occasion.

The first thought that the general ever shared with me was, Work them hard and tell them to always remember, "Team First!" After stressing the importance of "team," the general talked to our players about trust: You not only have to trust the man next to you, you also have to be aware that you're the man next to him—and he is trusting you to do your job.

The Friday night before we played the Jets in 2011, a local New Jersey high school teacher and minister named Gian Paul Gonzalez spoke to members of the team during our weekly chapel service. "Sometimes we've got to step up and be all in," he told them. "You have to be willing to say, 'I'm going to be all in and risk everything and bet everything.'" He then asked each player to sign a poker chip with their name and number, and keep it close to them as a reminder of their commitment. "All in," became a theme for us for the rest of the season; it was even printed on the towels our fans waved from the stands. The theme caught on in a way nobody expected and became an important motivational tool. It had a slightly different, but equally important, meaning to each player. Linebacker Michael Boley explained, "When you say 'all in' you should feel like you have nothing left when you walk off the field. Everybody's all in; mind, body, and soul."

For Kevin Boothe, "all in" was a perfect theme: "It's a mentality we took on toward the end of the season, when we had to win. It's about being willing to do whatever is asked of you, and even volunteering to do things that you normally wouldn't do."

Justin Tuck kept his chip on a mantel in his bedroom, where he would see it before he went to sleep and when he woke up, to remind him of what he had to give to the team. For the remainder of the season, until and including the Super Bowl, it represented the commitment we had made to each other to give everything possible. We were all in.

Sometimes motivation comes from unexpected places. The Giants organization has actively participated in the Make-A-Wish Foundation, in which seriously ill young people are granted an opportunity to live out one of their dreams, be it a trip to Disney or a chance to hang out with some of our Giants players. In November 2012, we had just come off two consecutive losses in which we hadn't played very well, and we were about to face a very good Green Bay Packers team led by Aaron Rodgers. The day before the game, we invited fifteen-year-old Adam Merchant, who had been fighting a rare form of non-Hodgkin's lymphoma, to attend our practice. At the end of the practice, Adam was asked to join our team huddle and say a few words. I didn't have the slightest idea what he was going to say, and in fact, I probably expected our players to give him the pep talk. Instead, Adam said later, "They sprung it on me [that] I was going to do the huddle. I didn't have much time to think about it, but I knew right away what I should say. 'Just play like the world champions you are.' "

Just play like the champions you are. That simple message hit home. "It's tough not to be inspired by something like that," said defensive end Mathias Kiwanuka. "He's a kid dealing with something we have no idea about. We can't put ourselves into his shoes. For him to want to spend his time with us, and for him to give that fiery speech was heartfelt. Everybody wanted to match the intensity of it."

We went out the next day and played the best game of our season, defeating the Packers 38–10. Thanks to Adam, we remembered to play like world champions.

While invited speakers can motivate the team, nobody speaks to the players more than I do. The leader of any team or business has to be visible and vocal. He or she has got to be seen and heard. They have to set the standards and reinforce them. The message has to be a culmination of everything else that has been presented, and it has to be heartfelt. It has to motivate the group to want to perform whatever task they are doing to the utmost of their capabilities.

I take a lot of time preparing my Saturday night remarks to the team. A lot of time. Once I decide on the message I want to deliver, I find the best way to do that. It's not always going to be a fiery pregame speech like the one Gene Hackman gave in *Hoosiers*. Each game is different and requires a different message. But it always will be informative, supportive, inspirational, and motivational. What I want to do is remind the team of everything we've emphasized all week in practice and in meetings, reinforce those ideas, and make the team confident that they are well prepared for this game. As I told my team the night before Super Bowl XLII, we would win if we demonstrated "pride, poise, team, and a belief in each other."

I'm a big believer in the use of inspirational quotes. I spend a lot of what my wife laughingly refers to as my free time searching for inspirational materials. I post the quotes in the locker room and I use them in my speeches. Quotes from people who have achieved the kind of success we are working toward reinforce the points we try to make. It doesn't matter what field these people come from; their message can be useful to anyone striving for success or facing adversity. Obviously not every quote is going to have meaning to every person, but they all help create a positive message. And when a particular quote does have meaning to a player it really can motivate him. It's important to know that someone else was in a similar situation—he or she was exhausted or down or depressed—and found a way to succeed.

Michael Strahan said that at first he paid no attention to the many quotes we hung around the locker rooms and used in our pregame talks. He thought my use of so many quotes was silly high school locker room stuff. As he explained, "He would quote anybody from General Patton to Mia Hamm.

When he first started doing it, everybody would roll their eyes and think, 'Oh no, not again.' But then I started reading them, and every once in a while one of them would strike me, and I'd think, 'Okay, I get that.' And eventually I was reading every quote and thinking, 'Yeah!' We all started looking forward to the next one, and if we didn't get a quote, we knew something was wrong. We needed that inspiration. It helped us get our minds set for that game. It absolutely helped put us in the best position to compete."

Michael once said that he would repeat some quotes to other people, a process he continued long after he retired from football, and still does now that has become a very popular TV host.

The quotes that I use come from books and movies. I get tips from people who know what I'm looking for. Many of the motivational quotes are from famous sportsmen, like boxing legend Sugar Ray Robinson, who said, "To be a champion you have to believe in yourself when nobody else will." Of course, like every other coach in the world, as well as people in business, I often quote Vince Lombardi, who spoke of all the characteristics necessary to win: "Unless a man believes in himself and makes a total commitment to his career and puts everything he has into it—his mind, his body, his heart—what's life worth to him?" and "Selfless teamwork and collective pride accumulate until they make positive thinking and victory habitual," and "Mental toughness is many things and rather difficult to explain. Its qualities are sacrifice and self-denial. Also, most importantly, it is combined with a perfectly disciplined will that refuses to give in. It's a state of mind—you could call it 'character in action.'"

But I also look beyond sports, quoting people such as the poet John Dryden, who wrote, "Let us lay awhile and bleed a little, and we will rise to fight again"; community activist Bertha Calloway, who said, "We cannot direct the wind, but we can adjust the sails," and Rabbi Lewis, who said, "Faith is about doing. You are how you act, not just how you believe."

MOTIVATION THROUGH EMOTION: THE POWER OF LOVE

Preparing a talk you're going to make to your team or organization is never easy. Every group you speak to is different, every situation is different. You have to speak directly to the needs of that specific group at that specific moment. What is it you want them to know? What is the message you want them to carry away when they walk out the door? I have never recycled a speech, I've never picked up something I'd said so many years earlier that no one would remember and repeated it. To figure out what I want to talk about I just look into my heart. I say what I'm feeling. My players know me well enough to know there is nothing phony about me. When I tell them something, I mean it. I don't think any of the people who were in that meeting room with us at the hotel the night before Super Bowl XLVI will forget what I said to the team.

The night before the Super Bowl four years earlier, I had spoken about pride, about how their lives will change forever after they've won a world championship. That night, we showed the team highlights over the song "Time of Your Life" by Green Day. But this was a different team, and it inspired a totally different feeling in me. The talk I gave was honest and sincere. It was what I felt in my gut that this team needed to hear from me. It may have been one of the most unusual pre–Super Bowl speeches ever given—especially coming from me. I think it surprised everybody. I had been through some football battles with this team—there had been a lot of rough moments—but we'd all got to that place, on that night, together, and that's what I decided I wanted to talk about. So we watched some videos of our big plays with "In the Air Tonight" by Phil Collins in the background, and then I began my six-minute address by reviewing the season and telling them how proud I was of every person in that room. We had gotten to the finish line together; now there was only one thing left for us to do. "Maybe what matters most is not only how we reach the finish line and why, but who crosses the finish line with us," I said. "We've talked about brotherhood. We've talked about being connected at the hip. Well, I'm telling you right now, I'm so very, very proud of this football team. You have been inspiring to a nation of people. Do you realize there are millions of people out there who you have inspired—who we have helped literally every day, who may be down on their luck, or perhaps life has dealt them a bad blow, who now, all of a sudden, because of this team, believe that anything is possible . . .

"I speak for the coaches when I say this; this is not just coming from me, but, I am so very, very proud of you, and I am so blessed, blessed to be part of this team.

"You all know about the Pyramid of Success that John Wooden built. The very top of the pyramid is the phrase 'Competitive Toughness.' . . . But later in life he said, 'Competitive toughness should be replaced by love.' With love, love—you guys have taught us what love really is. When you put it on the line the way you do every Sunday, when your ass is up against the wall, you have taught us what love really is. And I am man enough to tell you guys that I love you, and these guys [the coaches] all love you. They love you!

"Let's go climb this next mountain together. Let's climb this next mountain together, and let's be world champions against all odds. Let's be world champions."

I meant every word I said that night. *Championships are won by teams who love one another.* Love isn't used that often as a motivational tool, but it might just be the strongest one of all. It takes into account so many other significant factors: respect, dedication, commitment, gratitude, admiration, desire, fortitude, teamwork—all those things that are required for success that will come into play over a long season. As a player and as a coach I know how powerful the bond between player and coach can be. In business, that same strong bond can exist between any leader and those people he supervises. Doug Flutie's words are exactly what I felt as a player about my high school coaches or Coach Schwartzwalder and his staff at Syracuse, although he was talking about me when he said, "I didn't want to let Coach Coughlin down." But that bond should be just as strong for the leader. If your people do everything you've asked of them, if they've fulfilled the requirements of the system, then you have the same obligation to do everything possible not to let them down.

That 2011 team did everything the coaching staff had asked, and sometimes more. That team developed an extraordinary depth of character and, as much of a cliché as it is, refused to lose. We didn't just believe we would win; we knew it. There wasn't one person in the entire organization, not just the players and coaches, who didn't feel that we were all sharing a unique and very special experience. The only way to describe that accurately was love.

Motivation alone won't get you to the finish line. To get there you need talent, commitment, determination, and intelligence. But as Coach Tracy's kids learned, it is motivation that keeps you going until you've crossed that line—and as is so important to emphasize, it matters who crosses the line with you.

SIX

Hard Work Is Good Practice

We are what we repeatedly do. Excellence then is not an act, but a habit.

—ARISTOTLE

No one should be surprised when hard work results in success. That's the intention, that's the reason we spend all that time and effort. There may be great satisfaction in that success, but it should never be a surprise. John Wooden said, "I believe one of the biggest lessons of sports for dedicated individuals and teams is that hard work, really hard work, pays dividends. The dividend is not necessarily winning every game. The guaranteed dividend is the complete peace of mind gained by knowing you did everything within your power—physically, mentally, and emotionally—to bring forth your full potential."

And it is by becoming the best that you can be that you earn the right to win. Even when you're working by yourself, when you're lifting weights in your basement or studying plays late at night, when you stay late at the office or work on a beautiful weekend, you're really doing it for the whole team. A football team is only as strong as the fifty-third player on its roster. The success of a team, of any type of group, is going to be greatly hampered by even one person who is not willing to pay the price.

I take great pride in the fact that my teams work as hard or harder than our competition. That's not a secret. I tell people bluntly right at the beginning, If you want to play for me, you're going to work harder than you ever have before. When I walked into the training complex at Boston College for the first time, the team was in the middle of an off-season conditioning workout. I watched for a few minutes, and suddenly one of the players just got up and walked into the men's room. I followed him right into the men's room, questioned his commitment, and then dragged him out. I called the team together and told them, "My name is Tom Coughlin. I'm your new coach. I'm not here to make friends. I promise you this: When you leave here, everything in your life is going to be easier than this." Maybe they thought I was kidding.

PRACTICE IS PREPARATION

Motivational speaker John Di Lemme wrote a poem titled "Who Am I?" Two stanzas from it read:

*Half the things I do you might just as well turn over to me,
and I will be able to do them quickly and correctly.*
I am easily managed; you must merely be firm with me.
*Show me exactly how you want something done and after a
few lessons I will do it automatically*
*Take me, train me, be firm with me, and I will place the
world at your feet.*
Be easy with me and I will destroy you.

Who am I? I am habit!

Practice is the time and the place in which we build the habits that enable us to succeed. A successful performance is the result of a sustained effort to improve by following a regimen of deliberate, targeted activities, each of them designed specifically to optimize improvement in carefully selected areas.

In late June 2012 the New York Yankees invited me to throw out a ceremonial first pitch before a game. There isn't much to it: Just walk out in front of the crowd, stand on the pitcher's mound, and throw the ball to the catcher. This was the second time in my career that I had been invited to do this. I had seen other people walk out to the mound and bounce it to the plate or throw a wild pitch. My objective was to throw a strike. John Wooden told me that once he had been asked by the Angels to throw out the first pitch. I asked him how he'd done. "I bounced it," he admitted.

"Well," I said, knowing how much the city of Los Angeles loved Coach Wooden, "They wouldn't have booed you."

He just smiled.

I didn't intend to be booed. Two weeks before the ceremony Ed Triggs, my catcher, and I rigged a mound at our facility and I spent half an hour three or four days each week winding up and throwing the ball the sixty feet six inches from the pitcher's rubber to home plate. When the time came to throw it at Yankee Stadium, I threw a semi-fastball high and inside, "Close enough," I told the media. "I might have gotten the call."

At least I didn't bounce it.

Not too many people would have taken the time to practice for something like that. But I did. You earn the right to win on the practice field. Practice is the essential core of preparation. It's where a team builds its toughness. Practice may not make perfect, but there is a direct connection between the work you put in during practice and the results. The Aristotle of the gridiron, Vince Lombardi, used to tell his players that the habit of winning comes from the good habits instilled on the practice field. What happens in a game on Sunday is almost always determined by what we did the previous Wednesday, Thursday, and Friday. No one should ever put themselves in the position of doing something for the first time, or even the second time, when they're keeping score. To me it's senseless to go into any important activity without having spent all the time you can practicing to do it to the best of your ability. It's a really simple equation: The more times you do something, the better you're going to be at it. It doesn't matter what it is, you're going to do it better the third or the fifth or the twentieth time than you will the first time.

The three words that I absolutely guarantee have never been said at one of my practices are: "It's only practice." Only practice? There are people who feel that way, who think they should "save" their energy for the actual event, but those people won't be on my team very long. Practice allows you to acquire, develop, and refine the skills you need to succeed not just in football, but in any aspect of life. In an orchestra, for example, the trumpet player practices so he doesn't have to think about his finger placement during a performance. Actors rehearse. A quality performance is the natural extension of practice. The harder you work in practice, the easier the performance will be.

Practice sessions can be difficult. Everybody knows that. Nobody cheers for you in practice. A good practice is hard work. I've heard many players say that they play for free on Sunday, but they get paid for practicing. I do remind our coaching staff that we have an obligation to our players to use their time efficiently, and that the process for installing our weekly game plan should be as meaningful and vibrant as possible.

As Eli Manning said accurately, a good practice consists of the meticulous repetition of the same movements. Contrary to common belief, there is actually very little teaching that takes place during practice. The field is not the place for lengthy, detailed instruction or evaluation. The teaching takes place in the classroom both before and after we're on the practice field, and because of that we spend significantly more time in the classroom than on the field. The reality is that if you do something often enough, you get used to doing it without having to pause—even for an instant—and think about it. Do anything often enough and it becomes instinctive. Repetition is essential. On the football field things happen so quickly that a player has no time to think about what he wants to do or when he wants to do it; he simply has to do it. A split second can determine the outcome of a game. For example, the timing of a pass route has to be precise. Ideally, the receiver turns and the ball is right there waiting for him. That doesn't happen by luck or chance. It happens because the quarterback and the receiver have practiced that play over and over and over, until it has become instinctive. Quarterbacks and receivers who have played together for a while claim they can sense each other's movements. That bond exists only because of the time they've spent working together in practice.

A team is a combination of moving parts. We've all heard a winning team referred to as a "well-oiled machine." Practice is when you put in that oil. For a team to be successful, all those parts have to move in unison as they have been taught. One person out of sync is like throwing a wrench in the gears. The whole machine can break down. There is an old locker room slogan: You play like you practice. When a team is sloppy in practice, it tends to play ragged on Sunday, but when a team is sharp and energized and confident in practice, that also will be reflected on the field.

If people are going to make mistakes, practice is the place to make them. That's when those mistakes, or a lack of understanding or knowledge, can be corrected without it costing us a game. But there is no reason for anyone to make that same mistake twice. Practice is also the time to improve the fundamentals of technique. In an NFL season, improvement and learning is cumulative. While each week we emphasize the critical situations for the next game, we also work on many of the same things week after week. But in order for practice to be valuable, your people have to work as hard as they will play in the game. Some people believe they can give less than a complete effort in practice, then just crank it up on Sunday afternoon. We try to correct that impression. While no one is keeping score in practice, the coaching staff is watching, and sometimes making judgments.

But practices also provide an extremely useful opportunity for a leader to forge teamwork, evaluate talent, make the personnel adjustments that are necessary, and plan and correct. Just as we prepare for a game, in business, the more you prepare for a meeting, a presentation, a conference, even a sales pitch, the more successful it is going to be. While a lack of practice won't cause a presentation to be intercepted, it probably won't go for a touchdown either.

ORGANIZATION IS ESSENTIAL

To have value, a practice session has to be extremely well-organized. The goal isn't to spend a lot of time on the field, but rather to use the time spent on the field effectively. Contrary to a common belief, long practices are neither desirable nor particularly beneficial. For that reason, in order to be valuable a practice session needs to be well planned, disciplined, and completely thought through. I want my practice sessions to follow an up-tempo pace, complete with energy and enthusiasm. Our practices are regimented; they are scheduled minute by minute to make the most efficient use of our player's time. There is little or no time spent standing around waiting. During a typical practice session we'll spend no more than two hours on the field, during which each unit will go through as many as a dozen different drills. We use that time to refine individual skills, we practice playing together as a unit, and we expose our players to our upcoming opponent's strategies. There's a lot to get done, and if you try to accomplish everything that needs to be done in one or two sessions, you won't get it done. That will never happen. Perfection is what we're striving for, but perfection is an impossibility. However, striving for perfection is not an impossibility, and that's what we do. We go out, we get our work done, we get off the field.

You begin planning a practice session by determining what you need or want to get done. Once you've identified your objectives, you figure out how you're going to do it all. We make a schedule and we follow it. That's a given. Before practice begins, everyone knows what we're going to work on and when we're going to work on it. The more specific we make the schedule, the less time we waste. At Boston College, President Donald Monan, S. J, used to tell people, "Did you ever see one of his practices? It's like a military operation."

FOCUS

At RIT the players had to cross a small bridge to get to our field. The team rule was that once they crossed that bridge they had to have their helmet on and their focus had to be on football. Their daily world existed on the other side of that bridge. In Jacksonville we painted the "concentration line" on the floor leading out to the practice field, and once you crossed that line your focus was on doing your job, and only that, until you crossed that line going back.

During practice we prepare our people for as many of the situations that might happen both in our next game or at some point later in the season. At practice we work on the specific situations we may well see during a game. But usually we'll work on them only once during the week. As football demands that the learning of various situations be accumulative, the next week we'll do it again, and maybe we'll add or subtract something. And the week after that we'll do it again. It's an ongoing process, and the repetition builds quality. On Wednesdays, for example, we'll work on first and second down, kickoff return, punt, and field goal. On Thursday, third down and two-minute offense, punt returns, punt, kickoff, field goal, and field goal block. On Friday, red and green zone, goal line, short yardage, field goal block, and punt return. We schedule a block of time every week to work on each aspect of the game.

FUNDAMENTALS

At Boston College, Doug Flutie had a habit of taking a false step, an extra and unnecessary little step with his left foot, after taking the snap from the center. It drove me crazy. In practice I would stand behind him screaming over his shoulder, "Your footwork has to be exact!" Every day. "Your footwork has to be exact!" I wanted him to be absolutely perfect in practice, so playing the game would be easy. A meticulous sense of the importance of fundamentals is how I referred to this attention.

Almost any activity can be broken down into its parts. That

can include anything from throwing a forward pass to demonstrating a product. These are the fundamental skills that can be taught. It's obvious that the more parts that are performed correctly, the better the entire activity will be. I insisted that quarterbacks not waste a single step when dropping back; it doesn't seem that important, but that extra split second, or better balance, can make a difference in the outcome.

According to my good friend Ernie Bono, a five-feet-one-inch 140-pound running back who played football at Cheney State and later became a member of the board of directors of my charity, the Jay Fund Foundation, psychologists say that if you do something nine days in a row, it becomes a habit. I don't know how they arrived at that number; I've seen players pick up fundamentals in a day or two, and I've seen other players struggle with them for a long time. You can work your way out of bad habits and into good ones. Fundamentals have to be worked on every day in order for them to become second nature, then you do them naturally. The end result of repetition may not be perfection, but it certainly will be noticeable improvement.

PAY THE PRICE

Early in my career, especially when we were establishing the programs at RIT, Boston College, and Jacksonville, I became known, and was often criticized, for my tough practices. During my practices I don't want to ever see people standing around. I learned to run practices that way when I played for Ben Schwartzwalder at Syracuse. Coach Schwartzwalder was a square-jawed old paratrooper who had jumped into France on D-Day. He built his teams in his image. Everything we did he equated to some type of battle. Ben won the national championship in 1959 and produced great players like Jim Brown, Ernie Davis, Floyd Little, Jim "Bo" Nance, and Larry Csonka. His practices seemed to last forever; in fact, every practice was three hours long. Even when we were doing two-a-days in the summer, we worked three hours in the morning and three hours in the afternoon, always in full pads. We did a lot of contact drills; we hit each other in practice every day. We hit each other hard enough to make that tough man smile. In spring practice my freshman year I got tackled from the side and injured my MCL. I was writhing on the ground in pain. Coach Schwartzwalder walked over to me, looked down at me lying on the ground, and shook his head, "That's a shame," he said. "That'll teach you to cut back to the inside on a screen pass." Then he turned around and went right back to work.

It was the difficulty of getting through those practices that brought us together as a team. We had all gone through a really challenging time together. As a result of the work we did during the week, on Saturdays we physically manhandled almost every one of our opponents. And by the time we graduated, those of us who didn't love Coach Schwartzwalder definitely respected him. Eventually we realized how much he had taught us, not only about the game of football, but about dedication, perseverance, toughness, and teamwork.

At RIT I ran my practices the way I'd learned at Syracuse. I was tough on my players. They discovered they were capable of accomplishing more than they had thought possible. One big difference between RIT and Syracuse was that at RIT my players literally had to pay the price. We didn't have any scholarships, so everyone on the team was paying tuition. There were some players who felt my practices were more than they had bargained for and didn't buy into it. Some players quit, complaining it was too much for them. "I came to play football." Ken Wegner told me, "not be on the track team." He was ready to quit the team. I told him the same thing I told everybody else: He wasn't doing the work for me, he was doing it for his teammates, and for himself. This was his opportunity to become the best that he could be. Whatever he put into it, that's what he eventually was going to get back. "If you're quitting because you don't want to pay the price," I told him, "just remember: That's the way you're going to be the rest of your life. You should know that, and you should accept it."

The effort we put into those practices brought us together as a team. Everyone took great pride in our accomplishments as a team, and also in his own growth as a player and a person.

From just about our first day in Jacksonville, we had two-a-days in full pads, and then we ran. Jeff Lageman says about those early days: "He kicked our ass. The first year we had a team, that training camp, the only time we didn't have a two-a-day was the day after a game or when we had a mandatory day off. And we did conditioning every day at the end of the afternoon practice.

"He can put it to you. And that first year he did."

At Jacksonville, Tony Boselli recalled, "We never left a practice, or a game, relaxed. We probably practiced harder than anybody in the league. But, as a result, we had a close locker room, the one thing everybody had in common was that at some point you were mad at Tom. But when we started winning, we got it, we saw how all that hard work in practice paid off."

When I was hired by the Giants the players were well aware of my reputation for demanding a total commitment to success. Before our first training camp cornerback Will Peterson said, "I'm going to get myself in the best shape I can possibly get in. And I'll pray for the best."

PRACTICE IS A CHALLENGE, NOT A CHORE

"Fun" wasn't a word I had often heard associated with "practice." I didn't believe practices were supposed to be fun. But as I adapted in other areas in 2007, I also relaxed some of my rules about practice. We didn't work out in pads as often; sometimes we even cut practice a little shorter than scheduled. There is a point during the season where physical recovery becomes an issue. People were banged up and we didn't want to make it tougher for them. We were able to do these things with no loss of preparation, because we had veteran players who came to work prepared to do their job. We were able to adjust the workload and still accomplish everything that needed to get done. The players noticed. And once we started winning, those practices did become more fun. "Eventually it got to the point where we challenged each other," Michael Strahan explained. "It became a competition to see who could make the most plays, who could make the most tackles, who could just be the most disruptive. Not just in games, but in practice. We had drills, and in the drills we would put teams together, basically pick guys—'I want him. I want him'—and we'd go against each other in everything from warm-ups to drills. We were competitive in everything we did in practice, and it carried over to the games. When we got out there on Sunday it wasn't, 'I'm going to get five sacks.' It was like, 'I'll meet you at the quarterback.'

"Because of all the work we put in during the week, when Sunday rolled around, we didn't feel like anybody could mess with us, because when we all played together we knew we were better than anybody else. . . . The things we did during the week brought us together as teammates and friends, so on Sunday I wasn't just playing football; I was playing for my friends and for guys I felt were family. And that takes you a lot further than just doing a game plan or running around trying to tackle somebody. It actually put a purpose behind what you were doing."

I wouldn't go so far as to describe our practice sessions as fun; instead, I would call them professional and productive, which at times could be fun. When you're winning, anything can be fun.

THERE IS NO SUBSTITUTE FOR A WORK ETHIC

John Wooden pointed out accurately that "winners are usually the ones who work harder, work longer, and, as a result, perform better." If there is one thing that most great players have in common it is that they have a great work ethic. You don't have to tell them to do something a second time. They want to be better, and they are willing to do the work necessary to get there.

In 1993, at the end of my third season at Boston College,

we played undefeated and number-one ranked Notre Dame. A year earlier the Irish had beaten us 54–7. This was their final game of the year, they were on a seventeen-game winning streak and a victory would set them up for another national championship. We took a twenty-one-point lead into the fourth quarter, but they had stormed back to go ahead 39–38. With five seconds left to play, we took a time-out. I sent our placekicker, David Gordon, into the game to attempt a 41-yard game winning field goal. Usually I don't talk to the kicker before sending him into the game, but for some reason this time I stopped him, looked him right in the eyes, and told him, "David, I just want you to make solid contact with the ball. I know you can do this. You can make it."

Even though he'd missed two kicks from about the same distance in earlier games, I had confidence in him. I remembered looking out of my office window in the middle of winter at our snow-covered field. And day after day, there was David Gordon, outside in the freezing cold, shoveling snow off the field so he could work on his kicking. I knew how hard he had worked to be ready to make this kick. He had practiced and he had prepared. He had earned that opportunity to go for it.

He drilled the football right through the uprights to complete our upset of the number-one team in the country, 41–39. This was the first time Boston College had ever beaten

Notre Dame. It was a game, a day, an incredible team effort that none of us will ever forget.

Eli Manning was another player whose work ethic led directly to success. He took a lot of criticism from the media his first few years in the league. But I never doubted Eli Manning would succeed, because he had talent, and he works as hard as anybody I've ever coached. In high school, for example, he played on the school baseball team, and after baseball games, he would make his teammates stay around and run pass routes for him so he could get some football work in. From the day we drafted him, he came into the facility early and stayed late. He came in on our off days to look at tape and work on his conditioning. He came in during our bye-week. He worked out in the off-season. During the lockout, he not only organized workouts for the team, when those workouts were done, he went down to Duke University with two receivers to work with his college coach, David Cutcliffe, because he felt he could do more to prepare for the season. He wanted Cutcliffe to critique his form and work with him to improve it. Eli puts in the time, he makes a personal commitment to do the work, and he is never satisfied that he's done enough.

There's a reason for that. As he understands, "On the professional level, talent isn't enough. You need to tie it into a solid work ethic. In college I thought I was working hard and

I had some success, that's part of my nature, but once I got to the NFL I figured out that I wasn't working as hard as I thought I was. There is another level of preparation, and to get there you have to work at it. My rookie season Coach Coughlin made me draw up every blitz against the various protections and then consider the call I should make. That prepared me for the way I would have to prepare to succeed. Now it's me stressing to my teammates the importance of preparation. I hold my own meetings with the running backs on Thursday and the receivers and tight ends on Friday, just to make sure we're on the same page. Here's everything we might see, here's the way I might handle it, here's how I want you to respond. It takes time and effort from everyone, but that hard work is the price of our success.

"There have been a lot of very talented football players who had success at every other level because of their natural athletic ability, but they didn't have the professional career they might have had, because they weren't willing to do the necessary work. They didn't take their playbook home at night to study, they didn't take the time to ask questions, they didn't work on those things that needed improvement, they didn't show up in the gym or for the summer drills. When they needed that extra edge, they didn't have it."

Putting in those extra hours, working hard, will make a difference. I guarantee it. I've seen that happen too many times not to understand the value of it. And not just for high-profile players like Eli Manning. We signed wide receiver Keenan McCardell as a free agent in Jacksonville before the 1996 season. He had been picked by the Redskins in the twelfth round of the 1991 draft. He literally worked himself from a low-round pick into an All-Pro. He became a favorite of mine because of his work ethic—and because he was tough. Nothing was ever handed to him, so he knew that his only chance to succeed in the NFL was to out-work, out-perform, out-study his competition. He was always looking for perfection, and while other players may have had more natural ability, he had that x-factor. He could grasp what we were trying to do and transfer that from the classroom to the playing field. He wouldn't give anybody an inch; as a twelfth rounder, he'd had to work incredibly hard to get a job, and he wasn't going to let it be taken away from him. He'd spend hours studying tape of the player he was going up against. He played hurt; he actually insisted on practicing with a separated shoulder. He and Eli Manning came into the NFL with very different prospects, but hard work made both of them successful.

What I always look for in an individual is a self-starter, someone who doesn't need to be pushed to work a little harder or a little longer to get the task done to their own high standard. People who do this will succeed in any field.

THERE ARE NO SHORTCUTS

There are no shortcuts when giving your best effort. Success requires doing the job the best way possible, not the quickest way or the easiest way. Roger Staubach once said, "There are no traffic jams on the extra mile," pointing out accurately that not everybody is willing to make that extra effort. For example, although we follow probably 95 percent of the same practice schedule from season to season, and we keep it all in the computer, each year we start from scratch in developing our training program. Rather than just printing out an old schedule and making whatever minor adjustments I think are necessary, each year we start from scratch and make out an entirely new schedule. We approach it as if we're doing it for the first time. I will look at the old schedule as I write the new one, and it will be remarkably similar. I prefer to write it by hand, to make sure that I don't miss anything, and because when I do it that way it sticks in my mind. Doing it like this ensures that we don't fall into patterns and that we don't overlook anything that might be changed or improved. This is time-consuming stuff. Could it be done faster? Of course. Does doing it this way create additional work? Absolutely. Is it the most efficient way of accomplishing this task? No. But for me it is the best way to get it done. I'd rather get it done right than quickly. Efficiency may save you time, but it may cost you quality. I believe completely that if we're going to do this, we're going to do it right. And if it takes a little more work to do it right, then we'll do that work.

Hard work can make up for a lot of shortcomings. Our first season in Jacksonville we didn't have the depth of talent to compete with the better teams, but we did have the desire and the drive. The 1995 Jaguars were one of the toughest teams I have ever coached. Jeff Lageman later said, "Our margin for error was small, but we were probably the hardest working team in the NFL in 1995. I truly believe that nobody, nobody earned the right to win more than we did. I mean, we prepared, we prepared, we prepared. We conditioned like no other team in the league, and when we played our first game, against Houston, holy cow, we played them tight and had the opportunity to win. That game gave us belief in ourselves that year. We complained, but when we started getting results, all that hard work was a lot easier to take."

SACRIFICE

Winning requires sacrifice. That means putting in all the hours it takes to become the best you can be. In season coaches work fourteen to sixteen hours a day from Monday to Thursday, we spend Friday night at home, and Saturday we are either in a hotel or on the road. It isn't optional; those are the hours it takes to be able to compete. Doing our jobs the right way often means giving up other things that you might enjoy doing more, or forgetting about having any leisure time. It makes it difficult to pursue a hobby of any kind. There is no question that it affects your family. You miss some of the important events of life; I missed my brother's wedding, for example, and I missed some of my children's events; I missed socializing with friends because there was work that needed to be done. I am fortunate to have a wife who understands this and is tremendously supportive. It isn't just the coaches and players who are sacrificing for the good of the team: My wife learned many years ago that during the season she isn't going to see me very often. I'm going to be working. In fact, she laughingly has told all our kids that if anything should happen to her during the season, they should just put her on ice until the season's over, because she knows I'll be working too hard to deal with it. While we laugh at that, there probably has never been a better description of the life of a football coach's wife. During the season it seems like every minute is scheduled, and it appears that our priorities are job, then family. That's not entirely true. This is a family business, meaning that every member of a coach's or player's family has to be understanding of what is required. They have to buy into it. One of the reasons we formed the Leadership Council was to make sure that all of our families knew our schedule as far as possible in advance, so they could make whatever plans had to be made.

We treat wives and children as vitally important extended members of our organization. That's an important part of bringing out the best in your people. Everyone wants to believe that management is sincerely interested in them as human beings. You can't fake that interest. If you're not sincere, they will know it. You're going to have a more productive and enjoyable workplace if you are sincerely interested in your people's lives, not simply how they do their job. Before Super Bowl XLII, I reminded the team that they weren't just playing for themselves, they were also playing for all of those people they love who have contributed to our success. They will get to enjoy the warmth of victory too. When a parent or the wife or the child of a member of a Super Bowl–winning team walks into a store, they will be welcomed and respected as a member of a championship team.

AN OPPORTUNITY TO CHANGE YOUR LIFE

For a lot of players, practice will be the best opportunity they will have to change their lives. Practice is where you catch the attention of a coach and earn the opportunity to play. In the theater, stars can be discovered in rehearsals or in small roles and auditions. In the business world, the work someone does with a less important client can lead to greater opportunities. And in sports, it's what you do with each opportunity that makes the difference. One person who did take advantage of practice sessions and preseason games was wide receiver Victor Cruz, who earned his right to play in practice. He worked his way up from an undrafted free agent we brought in essentially to fill out our preseason roster to an NFL star.

There have been many players who first attracted my attention by their efforts when they thought nobody was watching them. Victor Cruz is a good example of that, because he seemed to come out of nowhere to become a key player on the Super Bowl XVLI team. At the beginning of the 2010 season we wanted to take eleven receivers with us to training camp. We had six receivers under contract and we drafted one, so we had to find the four best free agents to fill out the preseason roster. We started scrambling, just like every other team. We knew about Victor Cruz because he was a local kid; he had played at Paterson Catholic High School in Paterson, New Jersey, and at UMass. When we signed him for training camp as a college free agent, we never suspected he would play himself into an important role on the team.

He earned an opportunity to play in a preseason game by the way he practiced. He worked hard, he had natural ability, and he was able to translate what he was taught in the classroom and in practice onto the field. He earned an opportunity to get some playing time in a preseason game against the Jets. In that game he caught six passes for 145 yards and three touchdowns, winning a spot on our fifty-three-man roster. Unfortunately, early in the season he injured his hamstring and was out for the rest of the year.

He made the team in 2011 as our third receiver. After our starters got banged up he got a chance to play. On our first third down play of the season, he took his eyes off a good pass from Eli and just dropped the ball. In pro football young, undrafted players don't get too many chances to succeed. We weren't sure what we had in Victor Cruz at that point, so we signed a veteran to play that position. I think that's when Victor realized he wasn't on scholarship, that his spot on the roster was in jeopardy. He stepped it up in practice, and when Mario Manningham got hurt before an important divisional game against the Eagles, Victor got another opportunity. He had three catches for 110 yards, including 74- and 28-yard touchdowns while being covered by All-Pro cornerback Nnamdi Asomugha, and was awarded a game ball in our 29–16 victory. That was the beginning of a record-setting season for him. We want other young players to look at a Victor Cruz and understand that the same thing can happen for them if they do their work in practice and are willing to sacrifice.

While players are always being evaluated during practice, an occasional bad practice can be overlooked. David Tyree was a valuable player for us in 2007. He was a Pro Bowl special teams player; he was always prepared, he did his homework, he practiced hard, he was serious about getting better, and he had always had a positive attitude. Eventually he earned the right to play some downs on offense, primarily as a blocker on running plays. After other teams got used to the fact that when he was in the game he'd be blocking, we designed a series of plays for David that looked like his typical plays, but then he would slide off his block and become a receiver. We got very good production out of those plays: during the regular 2007 season he had four receptions. Going into the Super Bowl that season, David Tyree was our third receiver.

On Friday, two days before the Super Bowl, David Tyree had the worst practice you've ever seen in your life. Normally he was a very good practice player, because he used that time as an opportunity to show the coaching staff what he could do. But that day he couldn't catch anything. Balls sailed through his hands; they bounced off his shoulder pads. We were very concerned—we had included plays for him in our game plan. Too often a poor practice can lead to a poorly played game. I remember Eli putting an arm around him and telling him, "Don't worry about it." He was kidding at first, then he added, "We all know we can count on you."

The Super Bowl was a terrific football game. Early in the fourth quarter we called a play for Tyree, and he caught a 5-yard pass for his first touchdown of the season. Finally, with a little over a minute left in the game, we were trailing 14–10 but moving downfield. On third and five, we called a pass play. David Tyree was not the intended receiver. But when our pass protection broke down, Eli had to start scrambling. As the pocket collapsed around him, he somehow spotted Tyree 32 yards downfield. He threw it right down the middle of the field. The Patriots' Rodney Harrison, a very physical strong safety, was draped all over David. Somehow David managed to pin the ball against his helmet with one hand. Then he grabbed it with his second hand and went to the ground. There was no question it was a completed pass— good for 32 yards and a first down. It was one of the most amazing catches in NFL history, and it will be talked about as one of the great Super Bowl moments forever. That one bad day of practice made no difference when the game was on the line.

Lombardi once said, "Practice does not make perfect. Only perfect practice makes perfect." Waiting for a perfect practice is the coaches' equivalent of the search for the Holy Grail. I've spent thousands of days of my life at practices, and I don't think I've ever seen a perfect practice. I've never walked away at the end of a practice feeling that we were finished. There is always something that can be done just a little bit better, always another lesson to be taught, another play that should be repeated. And if you love what you do as much as I do, you're always looking forward to the next practice.

LEAD BY EXAMPLE

At my age I'm not much of a running back. I can't tackle, I can throw a little—but one thing I can do is lead by example. I can work as hard or harder than anybody in the organization. You don't have to be big or strong or even smart to work hard. It doesn't take talent to work hard, just desire. It's something anyone can do. You just have to choose to do it.

I know from experience that people in the organization are watching me, and noticing what I do, and will follow my lead. My attitude rubs off on everybody. Fortunately for me, working hard has never been a problem. I don't know any other way of living. I grew up in a family where a dime made a difference, and if I wanted spending money, I had to earn it. If there was a paying job I could do, I did it. I always had a lot of energy, I never could sit still. My grandfather trained horses, and when I'd go to the track with him, the old horsemen would sit around the potbellied stove in the tack room and tell stories. After listening for a little while I'd drift outside and run around the half-mile track. I couldn't help myself. I was always on the move, always working. The determination to succeed by working as hard as possible followed me to college.

When I played football at Syracuse I made up for my lack of ability with my determination. I used to tell people that I was small—but slow! I worked long hours to learn how to compensate for those things I didn't do well. At Jacksonville, the coaching staff had to take an annual stress test. We would run on a treadmill that got progressively steeper and moved faster. I'd make a point of going last, and before I started, I'd find out who had run the longest, and then I would do everything possible to beat that time. Professional athletes are competitive by nature. They will respond to a challenge. Tell a really competitive person that someone else is faster or smarter or stronger—especially in professional football—or better than them in any way, and they will look you in the eye and then go out and work hard to prove you wrong. We often try to set up competitive situations in practice, let people play a game within the game, like our weekly two-minute drill in which the offense competes against the defense. The result may not show up on any scoreboard, but this is a game that both the offense and defense really want to win.

There's a quote from the great wrestler Dan Gable that I read to the team a few days before Super Bowl XLVI that summed up the way I felt: "When I'd get tired and want to stop, I'd wonder what my next opponent was doing. I'd wonder if he was still working out. I tried to visualize him. When

I could see him still working, I'd start pushing myself. When I could see him quit, I'd push myself harder."

THE REWARD FOR HARD WORK

Teddy Roosevelt, another man I've often quoted, understood the value of hard work. As I've quoted him to my teams, "No man needs sympathy because he has to work, because he has a burden to carry. Far and away the best prize that life offers is the chance to work hard at work worth doing." That's key. Working up a sweat isn't enough; you have to work with a purpose. You can't just put in the hours, you have to fill them productively. And you've got to have a passion for what you're doing. Jack Youngblood got it absolutely right when he said, "You learn that whatever you are doing in life, obstacles don't matter very much. . . . If you want to do a job bad enough, you'll find a way to get it done." If you want to do a job bad enough.

As I've told my players every place I've coached, I was there to win football games, not popularity contests. There were people at every stop who thought I was too tough, too demanding. They didn't like my philosophy and they didn't like me. But when we started winning, players started buying into what I was selling. And eventually something far more surprising happened. Several of my former players, some of whom I'd butted heads with, came back and told me they loved me.

The first time that happened I had a hard time dealing with it. I wasn't ready for it and I didn't know how to respond. I've never been particularly comfortable accepting praise. It certainly was extremely rewarding and gratifying to hear someone I greatly respect like Doug Flutie say, "After playing for Tom, the way he runs his ship, the rest of my career was a cakewalk. Tom was so intense all week, practice was tougher than the game. I am grateful to have played for him. I love Tom."

Obviously, statements like that make me feel very good. They would make anyone feel good. But the fact is that people will eventually respect any leader who brings out the best in them, who makes them better, and who they know will always be there to support them when they give their best effort. When I thought about what they said, I understood that what they were really telling me is how much they appreciated what I helped them learn about themselves, and that they took great pride in what they discovered. It turned out that the lessons they learned in the locker room and on the playing field didn't apply just to football, but to every aspect of their lives. It's not always an easy realization, what I'm trying to give them. We signed free agent safety Antrel Rolle in 2010. For much of his first two seasons with the team, he was outspoken in his complaints about the way we did things, but after we won Super Bowl XLV he looked back on what it took for the team to accomplish that. "I always felt like he was trying to turn us into men," he said, but eventually he learned, "Once I took a step back, [I realized] he is not trying to turn us into men—he is trying to help us become better men."

The proof that our system works is that we win consistently. During the 2012 season several of our cornerbacks were hurt, and we were very thin there. Antrel had begun his career as a cornerback, so we decided to move him there until we got some of our people back. He embraced that decision, explaining, "One thing I like more than playing safety or my own goals, is winning. So whatever it takes to win, that's what I'm going to do. I like the role."

No team is going to win the Super Bowl every season. Only one team in the National Football League goes home satisfied. And no lawyer is going to win every case, no salesman is going to be successful with every client. But it is possible for every person to continually get better, to move closer to success. There is a tremendous satisfaction in knowing that you've put in the time and the effort to reach your objective, that you've sacrificed and practiced and prepared, that you've spent seemingly endless hours working when no one is watching you or encouraging you, and you see the results. Eventually there will be a reward. There will come a moment when you achieve your goal, when you get to that place you've been striving to reach. And you know how you got there, you can trace every one of those steps, you can look back on the work you've done and really feel the value of it.

When the team in the lead has the football at the end of a game, we use what is called "the victory formation." The offensive line bunches up, the quarterback takes the snap and kneels down, allowing the clock to run off the final few seconds. Every Saturday we end our practice with that victory formation. The message is clear: This is where we want to be at the end of the game.

Success isn't the result of luck, chance, or fate. Following this proven program won't guarantee success, but it will put you in the best possible position to succeed. It will build and reinforce your confidence that you are prepared to meet the challenges you will encounter on the path. It will help you become the best you can be, and that will be reflected in all aspects of your life.

And when you finally do reach your goal, it won't come as a surprise. Instead, it will come with the great satisfaction that you did all the work that was necessary to reach that point. You have, in fact, earned the right to win.

EPILOGUE

For me, at least, it has been vitally important to be involved in something outside my job and my family that makes a difference to other people. I can get extremely caught up in my work. To move away from it, to alleviate some of the stress and the pressure, I like to be with my children and my grandchildren, to play a little golf, even to take an annual trip. In my case, one of the opportunities I have to keep the rest of my life in perspective is working with a charity I founded, the Jay Fund Foundation. One of my players at Boston College was a young man named Jay McGillis, a wonderful person with a working-class background very similar to mine who gave everything he had on the field. Toward the end of our 1991 season he was diagnosed with leukemia, and he spent the next seven months in and out of the hospital. During that time I got to know his family very well, and I saw the strain—both emotionally and financially—it put on them. Jay McGillis died on July 3, 1992.

I wanted to find a way to make sure his spirit was never forgotten and to give meaning to his death. When I got to Jacksonville, we founded the Jay Fund Foundation, which raises money to help ease the financial and emotional burdens on the families of kids battling cancer. Just imagine how difficult it is for a parent to be dealing with the almost indescribable reality that their child is battling cancer while also having to face mounting expenses. Our mission is to assist families in that fight by providing comprehensive financial, emotional, and practical support, helping them to really be able to focus on their child's well-being.

My daughter Keli eventually became executive director of the foundation. We've given families more than $4 million in grants and now have a $5 million endowment fund. Jay Fund grants pay for such things as mortgage, rent, car payments, utilities, food, and the other normal household expenses that continue to add up. We also use our experience and expertise to help families figure out how to manage their financial lives during this crisis period, even providing a financial coach to help them devise a plan for moving forward.

We have several fundraising events annually to support this program. One of the reasons the Jay Fund Foundation is successful in fulfilling our mission is that it was organized and is run by applying the same broad principles that are outlined in this book. It required determining our objectives, designing a plan to reach those objectives, creating a structured organization, recruiting highly motivated people with good character—in this case many of them volunteers—paying close attention to details, and an awful lot of hard work by dedicated people.

While the Giants dedicated an entire championship season to learning how to finish, many people will find that the hardest thing they have to learn is how to start. Putting off starting a project or the pursuit of an objective is really very easy: All you have to do is nothing. But taking that first step on what may be a long journey, knowing that you'll probably encounter a lot of obstacles along the way, knowing it's going to take time and a lot of effort can take courage. There are no guarantees that by putting the lessons of this book into practice you'll achieve your ultimate objective, but I can promise that when you play the game with passion and heart, when you are sincere in attitude and intentions, when the love of competition and the difficulty of the challenge brings forth a superior effort good things will happen. No team wins the Super Bowl every year, but it is possible for every team to continually show improvement. I urge my coaches and players to never stand still. You're either moving upward a little bit or you're going the other way. You can't expect to go upward too quickly, but you sure can go down very quickly. Recognize that, and ask yourself what it is you really want to achieve—and what you're doing to get there.

As Andy Rooney pointed out, "Everyone wants to live on top of the mountain, but all the happiness and growth occurs while you're climbing it."

This book has given you the tools you'll need to climb that mountain. Go ahead, take the first step.

ACKNOWLEDGMENTS

Tom Coughlin

Any meaningful achievement in my life has been made possible by the support of my family, starting with my parents, Lou and Betty; my brothers and sisters; my wife, Judy, and her parents, Paul and Eleanor Whitaker; my children and their spouses, Keli and Chris Joyce, Tim and Andrea Coughlin, Brian and Susie Coughlin, and Kate and Chris Snee; and our starting eleven, our grandchildren: Emma, Dylan, Cooper, Shea, Caroline, Marin, Wesley, Brennon, Clara, Walker, and Ally Ann.

Professionally, it is one thing to have an organizational philosophy, a master plan, and a core set of beliefs. It is quite another to have the kind of special people it takes to implement and execute your designs with passion, commitment, and an uncompromising work ethic. I have been blessed to have worked with men and women who share my vision and dedication to being the best we all can be. It all started with my teachers and coaches as I was growing up and working my way up the professional ladder. As a head coach, I must credit our success to our players; assistant coaches; medical, video, and equipment support staff; the supportive Giants ownership of John Mara and his family; and Steve Tisch and his family; the collaboration with Giants general manager Jerry Reese and his player personnel staff; and the loyal and dedicated support of the fans. Special recognition goes to Ed Triggs and Chris Pridy, both of whom work with me every day at the Giants to plan our days and prepare our messages to the team.

Besides my faith, my family, and football, my other passion in life is our Jay Fund Foundation. Thank you to all who have contributed your time, your passion, and your financial support so that we can carry out the foundation's mission honorably and in the memory of the spirit of Jay McGillis, who passed away twenty years ago.

The mission of the Tom Coughlin Jay Fund Foundation is to assist children with leukemia and other cancers and their families by providing emotional and financial support to help reduce the stress associated with treatment and to improve their quality of life. www.tcjayfund.org

David Fisher

It was my great pleasure to know Tom Coughlin during his playing days. The opportunity to work with him now has allowed me to confirm that that the values and respect I saw in him as a young man have only been strengthened. My admiration and appreciation for Tom Coughlin, and those things he stands for, have also been heightened.

In addition, there are two people without whom this book would not have been completed. First is the great Pat Hanlon of the New York Giants, a truly amazing man who somehow manages to continue moving forward with a smile. His hard work, his gentle prodding, his eye for detail is greatly appreciated. As is the work of our editor Natalie Horbachevsky, who has moved us deftly thought the minefields of publishing, and always with professionalism and charm.

I also would be greatly remiss if I didn't acknowledge—with great appreciation—the creative and editorial input of our publisher Adrian Zackheim. For so many reasons this book would not exist without his vision, his guidance, and his hard work.

I would also like to thank Casson Masters and Scribecorps, whose lightning-fast and completely accurate transcriptions enabled this book to be written; our agent, Scott Waxman, who always seems to know just the right way to move projects to completion; and Sandy Montag, a total professional.

And of course I would like to acknowledge the many contributions of my wife, Laura, who has created a life for us, and an environment that makes it possible to complete impossible tasks, while still being the best yoga instructor in New York. And finally, I would be remiss not to mention Belle, the feisty dog, who was behind me, literally, every word of this book.